ALSO BY JACK BOWEN

*The Dream Weaver: One Boy's Journey
Through the Landscape of Reality*

*A Journey Through the Landscape
of Philosophy: A Reader*

IF YOU CAN READ THIS

IF YOU CAN READ THIS
The *Philosophy* of Bumper Stickers

JACK BOWEN

RANDOM HOUSE TRADE PAPERBACKS
New York

If I did have a bumper sticker
It would just say, "Jessica,"
Because I love how it sounds.
But I don't.
Instead I'm dedicating this book to you.
To Jessica,
For all of the reasons.

2010 Random House Trade Paperback Original

Published in the United States by
Random House Trade Paperbacks, an imprint of
The Random House Publishing Group, a division of
Random House, Inc., New York.

RANDOM HOUSE TRADE PAPERBACKS and colophon
are trademarks of Random House, Inc.

Library of Congress Cataloging-in-Publication Data

Bowen, Jack.
If you can read this : the philosophy of bumper stickers / Jack Bowen.
p.   cm.
ISBN 978-0-8129-8105-6
eBook ISBN 978-1-5883-6950-5
1. Aphorisms and apothegms.   2. Bumper stickers.
3. Humor—Philosophy.   I. Title.
PN6271.B59 2010
808.88'2—dc22   2009033154

Printed in the United States of America

www.atrandom.com

2 4 6 8 9 7 5 3 1

ACKNOWLEDGMENTS

In the "No author is an island unto himself" sort of vein, while this project began as a solitary venture, it grew into a massive project and an ongoing, intertwined conversation. And thankfully so.

Thank you to my resident experts for sharing your expertise—not only for making this book stronger, but for the great conversations that often resulted from your feedback: Judy Bowen, Louise Grotenhuis, Charles Hanson, Marie Lehman, John Mairs, Doug Munz, Josh Maisel, Caroline Paterno, and Kelly Wanser. Thank you also to Mark Newton and Mike Shore for providing such a great sounding board. And, as if I can ever thank you enough, Al Spangler for your unique blend of wisdom and advising.

Thank you to Menlo School for your continued support and encouragement of me as an author; I cannot imagine a better place to work as an educator. To our "Spring Good-Times Philosophy Reading Club"—Daisy Anderson, Eliza Bara, Nicole Fasola, Elitah Petty, Anjali Ranadive, Nicole Wemple—good times. And thank you to Brayden Fabris, Jack Suiter, and Brad Haaland for sharing your expertise in creating artwork needed to bring certain stickers to life. Finally, thanks to all of my "student voters" at the Stanford Great Books program.

And to our little community for your continued support—the McMullins, the Clarks, and Jessica Rose for the inspiring vistas where much of this book was written, Mamm Hudnall for all your help with the website, and all the families of philosophy students and water polo players who have helped celebrate this process, making philosophical discourse what it's meant to be: open discussion amongst genuine people sharing ideas. I'd have trouble listing by name all the water polo families who have encouraged me and discussed ideas with me and offered endless support—just know that in the same way you say that I provide an atmosphere for your sons to authentically grow, you reciprocate that.

The behind-the-scenes team has been nothing short of awesome. I repeatedly hear disparaging stories from authors about their publishers, editors, and agents, and I can only nod along politely, unable to connect. First, to my agent, Felicia Eth, you have been so much more than an agent and have truly made this process both smooth and enjoyable in every sense of the word. Your ability to convince me that my computer-crash/manuscript-loss was a *good* thing—and that it turned out to be true—was magic enough. Thank you for encouraging me to find my voice. Thank you to my editor, Christina Duffy. I have really enjoyed getting to know you and sharing ideas with you. Your candid advice throughout the writing process has been invaluable. And to the entire staff at Random House involved with the book—from the art department, who allowed my input throughout the process, to the eagle-eyed production editor, Margaret Benton, and the marketing and publicity duo of Barbara Fillon and Kathleen McAuliffe—it has been an honor being affiliated with such a world-renowned publisher, and even more so to work closely with you.

Lastly, to my favorite anthropologist and the person who really encouraged me to write from my heart: Jessica. I have such fond memories of rushing home to share that day's writing with you: discussing the ideas, agreeing and disagreeing, pushing further; listening to you subtly yet firmly share where you thought I'd fallen short; and celebrating the moments when I really got it right. I had no idea I'd married the best editor in the world just a year ago.

CONTENTS

GOD AND RELIGION
The Supernatural, the Natural, and the *Extraordinarily* Natural

"THE FISH BOWL"— ⟨×⟩, *Etc.*

KNOWLEDGE
What You Don't Know *Can* Hurt You

ETHICS
Two Rights Make a Right

LANGUAGE
A Sticker's Worth 1,000 Words
. . . .**155**

POLITICS AND SOCIETY
You're Right to Pursue Happiness
. . . .**167**

THE BIG QUESTIONS
Is That Your Final Answer?

INTRODUCTION:
IF YOU CAN, READ THIS

In today's espresso-to-go, Tweeting, five-minute speed-dating, sound-bite culture, the bumper sticker continues to thrive as a means of expression. As author and cultural commentator Rick Shenkman writes, "If an idea cannot be expressed on a bumper sticker you can probably give up any hope that it will ever attract much support." Not even needing a physical car anymore, over 23 million Facebook users employ this virtual vehicle's "Bumper Sticker" app to make their views heard in typical pithy, catchy, clever bumper-sticker fashion. By their very nature, bumper stickers spark controversy and impart insight. Agreeable, commonplace slogans just don't sell well; we could imagine the bumper stickers "Abortion Is NOT Okay! But It's Okay Sometimes Too!" and "The Sky Is Blue-ish" hardly flying off the virtual shelves.

Not surprisingly, the simplistic style of bumper sticker–style commentary often leaves much to be desired. A single snide, sarcastic comment likely contains a kernel of truth, but it unavoidably ignores the richness of most any topic. Like a picture, a good bumper sticker may also be worth at least a thousand words, but any important issue merits much more than that.

Peanuts cartoon creator Charles M. Shulz once commented, "There's a difference between a philosophy and a bumper sticker." To some extent this rings true, as most "philosophies" and paradigms and zeitgeists (and all pedantic synonyms for such things) penetrate much deeper than the average eight-word bumper sticker. But a good bumper sticker also provides a great springboard for delving into these rich ideas. In the vein of the self-reflecting bumper sticker "My Manifesto Doesn't Fit on This Bumper Sticker," we really just need to sit with the bumper-sticker owner over a cup of coffee and explore what's really going on behind the scenes—and maybe bring our neighborhood philosopher along to share relevant insights.

The odds of getting one of these drivers to engage in civil discourse may prove challenging. According to a 2009 study by Colorado State University researchers, drivers of cars displaying bumper stickers exhibit more "road rage" than those without. Apparently, anyone who feels the need to share their thoughts with— or more accurately, *force* their thoughts *on*—others also tends to express their disapproval at your lack of speed in the fast lane. It turns out that the message of the bumper sticker doesn't matter: both the "Practice Random Acts of Kindness" and the "My Student Beat Up Your Honor Student" sticker owners will more likely sound an angst-ridden horn blast than another with a plain ol' naked bumper.

Bumper stickers don't just affect the drivers of cars. In recent years, numerous reports have highlighted people being fired—or hired—for their bumper stickers, pulled over, gestured at, and even chased down. In Oklahoma City in 2009, a man was pulled over for his "Abort Obama Not the Unborn" display on his truck bumper. The police confiscated it despite the driver clarifying that the statement was only a response to Obama's overturning the partial-birth abortion bill, and that his meaning of the verb "abort" did not imply "kill" but more closely resembled "terminate." In true partisan form, a Georgia police officer issued a $100 ticket to a woman for her "Bushit" bumper sticker. Though not even an actual word, the Orwellian "Thought Police" interpreted it as "lewd." (We can imagine the woman responding, "That's total bushit.")

And so it brings us to the first bumper sticker—the "If You Can Read This" Collection. It introduces the infamous "if," and with "if" comes its partner in crime, "then." It gets readers hooked—"If *you* can read this"—and then shows them what they can learn or do, or might be in danger of. "Hmm, I *can* read this. And since I'm one of the lucky ones—right place, right time—I'll keep reading to see what I can discover." . . . *Then You're Not Paying Enough Attention to Your Driving.* Lesson learned.

This crafty bit of grammar, aptly referred to as the "if-then" clause, is the driving force behind the power of these popular bumper stickers. Since "you" *can* read "this," then you're halfway to gaining potential insight. Of course, the then-clause must properly connect, unlike with the following two bumper stickers that likely aren't both true:

. . . *Then You're Too Smart to Vote Republican*
. . . *Then You're Too Smart to Vote Democrat*

By providing an easy "if-statement," passersby and other drivers become motivated to see what follows the ensuing "then." It's like asking rhetorical questions of readers to get them involved instead of talking *at* them. Take the following two versions of the same argument:

Telling: You can't get something from nothing. God couldn't have created everything because something would have been needed to create God. So God doesn't exist.

And,

If-Then Asking: If you can't get something from nothing, *then* how could God come to exist?

(St. Augustine once commented, "God was creating hell for people like you who ask such questions!" when asked what God was doing before creating something, so be careful.)

While both statements make the same point, the second invites readers to "figure it out" on their own. It's similar to the common advertising ploy to engage zoned-out television viewers: "Bigger is better. Burger King's burgers are bigger," runs the text, with images of the perfectly made BK burger contrasted with a cardboard-looking burger of that "other" joint. They leave it to the reader to distill the secret hidden logic behind the ad, thus solving the riddle of hamburger goodness themselves—"Wait a minute, *if* bigger is better and theirs is bigger, then *theirs* is better. I solved the riddle."

The beauty of the if-then clause is that it forces people to engage, to drive up a bit closer. To *look closer.* Which is exactly what "*If You Can Read This*" gives the reader the chance to do. And in our case here, readers can avoid the fear that once they can see the tiny print following the text "If You Can Read This . . ." it won't say something like other bumper stickers that follow with "You're in Range" (with a bull's-eye next to it), or "I Can Slam On My Brakes and Sue You." You're free to look as closely as you want. Encouraged to do so, actually.

The "if" clause of the "If You Can Read This . . ." bumper sticker is somewhat redundant. One could really insert "If you can read this" before every statement. Instead of "Imagine World Peace," it could read "If You Can Read This, Imagine World Peace." It's right up there with "If you *can't* read this" preceding a bumper sticker; sort of a variation on that old philosophical riddle "If a bumper sticker is funny in the forest and no one's there to read it, is it funny?" If you are reading "this," then you're reading it, *ipso facto.* It's like asking someone if they're awake, and in the same category as putting Braille on drive-through ATMs.

So with the if-clause now safely in place you can rest assured that there's something more than the upside-down instruction "Then Roll Me Over" to follow. Look closer. Get engaged. The bumper stickers in this book can all be found on the bumpers of cars throughout the country, or at your favorite online boutique. As another crafty bumper-sticking grammarian invites us,

IF YOU CAN, READ THIS

IF YOU CAN READ THIS

REALITY
It's Not Just Science Fiction Anymore

DON'T LABEL ME

We can pretty much blame this whole labeling problem on Plato. While he was certainly well intentioned, in the end he may have created more problems than he solved. Put simply, Plato attempted the most intensive labeling campaign known to humankind. He suggested that all individual things relate to, or participate in, their respective general class—what he called the universal "Form." Take the simple case of chairs. For Plato, every chair exemplifies the essence of *chairness,* which allows us to label such varying objects as backless wooden stools, and metal seats with backs, and legless, backless beanbags all as *chairs.* This eradicates the chaos of there being thousands of different things, and puts in their place just one sort of thing. Since they share the same label they *must* share some common trait.

For the most part, our minds aren't built for such time-consuming ventures as thinking and introspection—instead, a quick glance, assigning of a label, and moving on to the next task better serves our primary interest: survival. This natural propensity to categorize begins in children as young as one year old, and for good reason, as a child's ability to correctly label "hot" and "not hot" serves as a helpful survival mechanism. Burn me again, shame on me for not properly labeling. Our brains are great survival machines, yet poor truth detectors. In our long evolutionary history, the quick-footed cousin escapes the pursuing lion while the deep thinker is removed from the evolutionary playground, likely thinking all the while how unfair life is. Labeling allows us to *divide and conquer,* which certainly beats the survival strategy of *nit-pick and surrender.*

Author and "Scientist of Uncertainty" Nassim Taleb intuits the deeper problem with our habitual labeling, in that it "makes us think that we understand more than we actually do." He suggests that many of us have simply been referencing the wrong "user's manual" for our brains. This causes various problems. On the one hand, it impedes our ability to accurately view our surroundings. In our habit of incessantly labeling, we wrongly assume that these labels actually exist in some way, as part of the world. Additionally, this practice deadens our creativity. Boxing up various individuals and objects makes it harder to think outside of that so-called box. Harvard psychologist Ellen Langer refers to this as being "trapped by categories." For example, an auto mechanic sees just another spring, while his wife looking in on him, free of his constructs of labels, sees a toy—thus, the famous Slinky was born. And lastly, in treating everything as an example of one universal class or label, we miss out on the beauty in the fringes of uniquely constructed items, or, more important, the unique quirks and character traits of individual people. The antique shop's set of bowls have their own individual flair while the department store's set are all the same, and are just like those of your neighbors, and their neighbors down the street. Where's the beauty in that?

The problems run deeper than those of a private nature, such as one's viewing the world incorrectly or lacking creativity. Labeling others affects both how we treat them and how they see themselves. An MIT study had their students rate a visiting professor, though before he lectured they each read a short bio of him—half the class reading that he was "a very warm person" and the other half, "a rather cold person." Not surprisingly, their post-lecture reviews of him almost exactly reflected the prejudices of the fictitious labels. And most teachers are familiar with the Pygmalion Effect in which others behave according to the labels assigned to them. As the infamous exercise of one elementary school teacher shows, when students are told that having blue eyes relates to greater aptitude, the "blueies" outperform the "brownies." Yet, when the teacher announces the following day that she mistakenly switched the categories, the performance of the "brownies" increases accordingly.

Clearly this labeling business, while often practical, can cause great conflict. Fortunately, the ancient Greek philosopher Eubulides of Miletus provides us with another option, highlighting the inexact nature of these human-made categories. Writing during the same time as Plato, he asks us to agree that a certain pile of sand constitutes a *heap*. Upon his removing a single grain, we unanimously concur that it remains a heap, since obviously, *subtracting a single grain from a heap can't make it a non-heap*. Clearly, though, by that logic he could repeatedly subtract a grain until only a barely visible few were left—certainly not a heap's-worth. This example forced the recognition of the fuzziness of language and of labels.

To compensate for this deficiency of the traditional either/or binary logic, in 1965 UC Berkeley computer scientist Lotfi Zadeh introduced "fuzzy logic." This allowed mathematicians and others to provide more pragmatic quantitative descriptions, thus avoiding the pitfalls of pigeonholing (and it also allowed us to call them "fuzzy"). For example, placing a lit match in an *empty* gas barrel should do no harm; but knowing the barrel was .9 empty provides a much more accurate description. So instead of labeling a sand-grain collection as a heap/non-heap it could be considered a .7 heap, and so on with labeling people as introverts, as children, as good or bad—because no one truly maintains all of one quality, and forcing people into such black-and-white categories doesn't let the beauty of their respective grays shine. Or as popular television show composer Matt Bowen sings, "If you see the world in black and white / You're missing out on all the beautiful colors."

While this brings us closer to an accurate description of the world, it introduces a new practical challenge. Who gets the children's ticket price at the movies, .6 children and younger? The heap problem rears its head again as it forces us to distinguish between a .9 child and a .8, and it can't be just a matter of a day, an hour, or a minute.

At the very least, an awareness of our habitual labeling can help overcome some of the personal and interpersonal angst that results, often unknowingly. And a balance of Plato's Chairness and Eubulides' Heaps might just provide a more accurate view of the self and the world around us. Because if the only tool one has is a hammer, then everything really does start to look like a nail. So go to the store and use the labels for that soup you'll be serving in your antique bowls—though just realize that while the cashier who sells it may ask, "Did you find everything okay?" just like all the others, they're also a little quirky, and somewhat introverted, and a tad childlike just like you.

SIZE DOES MATTER

The same-sized "Large" soda of just ten years ago has since become a "Small." Actually, most fast-food chains have stopped even offering "Small" as an option, starting the bidding at "Medium"—or in the case of Starbucks, at a "Tall" and ending with the elusive "Venti" (Italian for "twenty," in reference to the number of ounces you get). 7-Eleven quickly surpassed everyone with their initial 32-ounce "Big Gulp"—three cans' worth of cola in one "serving"—only to soon dwarf that with their 44-ounce "Super Gulp" and the now 64-ounce "Double Gulp." This transformed their initial offering into a mere "Gulp," and dwarfed the initial McDonald's "Large" into a mere thimble's worth of the sugar-acid-caffeine elixir now overtaking other healthy options such as milk and water. Not to be outdone, ARCO offers "The Beast," coming in at 88 ounces, and causing cup-envy for all other pushers—Ronald McDonald ran out to buy a Hummer in order to compensate for his mere 42-ounce cup served to customers asking to "Super Size It."

Most of us intuit the objects and the space they occupy as absolutes. If you held a Tall coffee and then swapped it for a Venti, with you and your hand as an absolute, fixed reference point, the cups would appear to nearly double in size. As Isaac Newton suggested, a set frame of reference must exist to allow motion to be possible—if you're moving at sixty miles per hour and everything else around you is also, in the same direction, then what's the point? Thus, Archimedes held that if he could find just one fixed, immovable point, he could move the earth.

German philosopher Gottfried Leibniz demonstrated the incorrectness of this idea, thus anticipating Einstein's theory of relativity. He has us imagine another universe *exactly* like our own that exists simultaneously yet with one small difference: everything has been shifted five feet to the left. If this were the case, all agree that there would be no conceivable difference between the two universes. Since shifting everything five feet to the left truly does not matter, then what *does* matter is not where the things are, but where they are *relative* to everything else.

Returning to the philosophical playground, imagine now that every day everything doubled in size. So while your foot doubles in size, so does your shoe. And while your shoe is nine inches long, the ruler with which you measure it also doubles and thus the space between the end and the "9" doubles as well. As in the previous case, you would not discern this monumental change, thus demonstrating again the importance of *relative* size. Just imagine what that Venti latte would be like—it's a good thing your stomach would be doubling in size along with it.

But in our current state of affairs, not *everything* doubles in size. As other bumper sticker wisdom surmises:

IS THE WORLD GETTING SMALLER OR ARE WE JUST GETTING FATTER?

With America's obesity crisis, we may just be able to do the unthinkable here and actually link the relativistic view of space together with our previous discussion of soft-drink expansion. It may be no mistake that "size envy" explicitly mentions the sixth of the seven deadly sins. In our case here, it directly relates to the second sin, gluttony, conveniently derived from the Latin *gluttire,* "to gulp down"—one fast-food chain is not only envious of another's large cups, but this envy is driven by the gluttony of their customers. It is indicative of our culture of overindulgence and our need to constantly want more than we have, even when what we have is more than sufficient.

In 1978, economist Richard Easterlin conducted a survey among adults. He asked them to pick items from a list that they "Would like to own" and then, on that same list, items they "Currently own." Sixteen years later, he corralled the same group and asked them the same questions with the same list. While they had nearly unanimously acquired all of the items on their respective "wish lists," instead of being satisfied they developed new items on the list previously not desired during the initial survey. Termed the "hedonic treadmill," it has become clear to economists and "happiness experts" alike that "more" does not necessitate "better."

Much of this has led to the concern that a focus on GDP—gross domestic product—as the primary indicator of a country's well-being has sidetracked us from what we really want, taxing the environment along the way in our incessant push to produce. Senator Robert Kennedy once highlighted that the GDP counts *products* like napalm and nuclear warheads, jails and cigarette advertising, but not children's health and quality of education, nor the strength of marriages or the compassion and joy felt by the citizens. He reminds us that the GDP "measures everything, in short, except that which makes life worthwhile." Instead, argues Princeton psychologist Daniel Kahneman, we could abandon this in exchange for the less quantitative but more accurate designator GNH—Gross National Happiness. We could gulp down fewer ounces of soda, trade in the hedonic treadmill for an actual jog in the park, and exchange products for happiness.

With a high GNH, we can imagine that the good ol' six-ounce cup of coffee of yore will suffice and that maybe size does matter after all—relatively speaking, of course.

WHY DO PSYCHICS HAVE TO ASK FOR YOUR NAME?

Probably because there's no such thing as psychic power. And because the more questions they ask, the more information they get, and the more knowledgeable they appear to their vulnerable victims. Though maybe it's because the person paying the money only wants to hear what they want to hear, regardless of the process.

Winner, winner, winner. As *Skeptic* magazine editor Michael Shermer notes, "Talking to the dead is easy. Getting the dead to talk back is hard."

A psychic was hired to write a specific reading unique to *you* the reader of *this* book in your hands. As one of the top psychics in the world, she knew who would buy each book (obviously) and thus could easily pinpoint your future—and don't worry if you borrowed/stole this book, the psychic knew you'd do that and acted accordingly. (Given that this reading would typically cost you twice what you paid for the book, I hope you find it a valuable gift.)

You are a thoughtful person to whom relationships are very meaningful. While you can be quite reserved, if with the right people you are rather outgoing. You know many people, but you have a core group of friends who play a big role in your life. Continue to explore those friendships. Keep your eyes open for opportunities arising in the next nine months to make a positive move in your current schooling or career. This will allow you to focus on your romantic life. Trust yourself and give your romantic relationship time to progress the way it was intended. You are a very lovable person. And allow yourself that time to read good books and to relax as this will be your important way to connect with the cosmos.

You likely noticed another tactic of the successful psychic: Make universally relevant, extremely general claims. Even contradictory claims to cover all of the bases, such as being both reserved *and* outgoing. Include schooling *or* career to let the reader choose which fits them. Since they're reading a book, mention how much they like reading books. And imagine instead that you *had* paid to read this and *expected* to discover truths about your life—you would make sure to find them. After all, we sure hate to be duped.

But who really listens to psychics anyway? While it's hard to get a straight answer from any individual, someone is paying the *billions* of dollars that phone psychics bring in every year. All this despite any real proof or explanation. Except this one, from "psychic" Sylvia Browne—you may have seen her on afternoon talk shows counseling us on tragedies, attempting to solve murder cases, etc.—who earns $850 per thirty-minute phone call and explains that she can "psychically reach into your soul, pull out your chart, and then recite back to you those things you have already planned for yourself." Of course you don't need to be present for her to do this, as she is "just as good over the phone as in person." "Okay, before we get started, will that be Visa or MasterCard?" Really, you have to ask that?

Yet were we to *foresee* the accuracy of her next reading, if it resembled her 2005 performance we would have to predict she'd do no better than 30 percent correct. Interestingly, two fourth-grade classes at Heritage Hall Elementary School in Oklahoma City scored nearly 50 percent on the same predictions—exactly what we would expect from the coin-flipping-style guesswork of a psychic.

So maybe this is the new direction for educational fundraising—the schools could certainly use an extra few billion. The trick, of course, is educating them so they don't leave school to join the masses in which over a third believe in astrology, over half in ghosts, 75 percent in angels, and upward of 80 percent who claim to believe in miracles. Suspension of disbelief and imagination are important, but not so important that kids leave the movie theater thinking they can fly like Harry Potter, or cast psychic spells, for that matter.

UFOS ARE REAL

True: sometimes an *object flies* through the air that is *unidentified* by some people—hence, UFO. In January 2009, two New Jersey residents put together a contraption of helium balloons and flares and set it into the night air. That bastion of intergalactic news, Fox News, spent a considerable amount of time interviewing a local pilot and his wife in a report, "Folks in New Jersey believe they saw UFOs." They finished the segment with one of the "America's Newsroom" analysts noting, "They are the most credible UFO-guests I think I've ever seen. And from New Jersey, not from the middle of nowhere like sometimes it is." Additionally, these balloons made it onto the History Channel's *UFO Hunters* program where "expert" Ufologists such as the publisher of *UFO Magazine* gave definite commentary that the objects could not be flares or anything else man-made. The local airport control towers were also contacted, but *nothing* showed up on the radar—alien ships impervious to human radar systems. UFOs are definitely real, it's just sometimes hard to tell if they're balloons, Chinese lanterns, or ships containing actual aliens out on a joy ride.

As with most things that are "out of this world," one also has to flip the "I'll have to see it to believe it" adage on its head, adopting something more along the lines of St. Augustine's defense of Identified Unseen Beings (IUBs), "If you don't believe it, you won't understand it." Thus the bumper sticker,

I WANT TO BELIEVE

often leads to the purchase of

I BELIEVE IN UFOS

only years later. If you'd like to see a flying saucer, belief is a great place to start, as the 33 percent of Americans who believe that aliens have already visited earth can tell you. The real question is, what leads one to buy the bumper sticker "UFO Pilot"—at the least, the pilot should be able to identify the object he's purportedly flying.

Following the 1977 film *Close Encounters of the Third Kind,* alien abduction stories sharply increased. A majority of the profile sketches of aliens drawn by those purportedly snatched up during their late-night TV watching have an uncanny resemblance to the respective extraterrestrial star *du jour,* be it the earlier Buck Rogers cartoons or the more current *X-Files.* And oddly, all of these resemble one other creature: humans. But as our predominant skeptic Michael Shermer notes, "Of the hundreds and hundreds of millions of species, only one has become a bipedal primate. The chances of that happening anywhere else in our solar system, in the galaxy, and in the cosmos is virtually zero." Since we are so very special, any other super-special being in the cosmos should look like us too.

Okay, so we have no direct proof of aliens, but that shouldn't stop us. Some argue that indirect evidence exists right here on earth, in the Great Pyramid of Egypt. The argument, in simple terms, goes like this: This building is so big that humans couldn't build it and the only other possibility is aliens. While it certainly seems a bit shortsighted that humans couldn't stack blocks on top of each other, there is also no evidence of any alien technology, nor a fossil record of any sort. Pro-alien advocates support their claim noting that the height of the Great Pyramid multiplied by one thousand almost exactly equals the distance to the sun—this couldn't just be mere coincidence, they say, and so must be a message sent from the aliens or proof that they engineered such precision. Keeping the adage "I'll have to believe it to see it" fresh in your mind, you can find any correlation you desire if you look hard enough: the height of the Great Pyramid divided by the height of football legend Jerry Rice equals approximately 80—the exact number on Jerry Rice's uniform. Maybe Jerry Rice had something to do with building the pyramids.

UFOs are predominantly seen by farmers and families living "in the middle of nowhere" and never by astronomers and scientists constantly searching the cosmos with the most powerful observation tools available. For twenty-five years, the SETI Institute (Search for Extraterrestrial Intelligence) has conducted actual scientific research in pursuit of discovering extraterrestrial intelligence. With 100 billion other galaxies, each with 400 billion stars like ours, the probability of some life existing is thought by many to be quite high. Though with the nearest galaxy 2.5 million light years away, getting to them will take some time. Just like when we view our closest star we see it as it was over three years ago; you can do the math regarding what we would see of other galaxies. Just imagine what they would see, looking back at earth circa 2.5 million years ago. Hard to imagine their motivation for visiting the place that present-day New Jersey currently inhabits. And what would they even do on their spaceship for 2.5 million years, assuming a ship could ever travel at the speed of light?

Just be patient. Looking around for fifty years isn't that long. And look a bit closer at all of those flying objects and you can probably identify them, at the least making them mere FOs.

IT'S NOT A SMALL WORLD. IT'S THAT THERE ARE SO MANY OF US.

It's often been said, "What a *small* world we live in." But what would it mean for us to live in a *large* world? Or even a medium-sized world? We can't compare our world because it's the only world we know.

When we play the "It's a Small World" game, we forget just how small we have made our world to begin with. We never take a random sample of the 6.8 billion people, as if dragging our fingers blindly through the World Phone Book, landing it on two people's names. Instead, we whittle away our world into tiny pockets even before playing the game. Take the oft-given example of seeing someone on an airplane "randomly," as they say. You have already narrowed the demographic immensely: the two hundred people seated around you all have the financial wherewithal to fly, the interest in doing so, and are either from or visiting the same place as you.

And the opportunities for a "success" in this game are much more immense than we consciously realize—you're not looking for a *specific* person to match, but *any* person, connected in *any* way. When you board the plane you don't speculate, "I wonder if I'll see the girlfriend of the guy who sold my son his house a year ago?" Most people have a very wide-reaching net to cast. Imagine a father of two traveling from his hometown with his wife. This couple belongs to five different social groups and clubs each containing hundreds of members, they both work in different industries, participate in a community church, have a core group of neighbors, and went to different high schools and universities. And their children—also part of their net—both are married, with the four amassing a combined two thousand Facebook "Friends" alone, each with their extended families, universities attended, workplaces, interests, etc., etc. . . . The list goes on and on. So in this little world lurk *a lot* of winning combinations. Join that with the fact that not only does the father play this "Small World" game frequently—he goes to parties, flies, shops, etc.—the people on his "list of winning connections" also play a lot. One of the biggest oversights we make in this area of magical Disneyland-style small-world-after-all gamesmanship is that we overlook the "failed" attempts, rarely stopping to think, "Geez, I flew from San Francisco to Seattle and didn't know anyone." In addition, we fail to account for all of the flights our respective list-members take and yet never achieve a successful encounter. With all of the opportunities for a winning match, we should be surprised at how *few* of these serendipitous, coincidental encounters occur.

This game we play is pretty much dopamine's fault. This brain chemical regulates emotions, causes our natural highs in areas of uncertainty, and can almost singlehandedly take the blame for gambling addictions. We get a little shot of it every time we have a victory amid randomness or find a pattern even where there is none. Neuroscientist Read Montague explains, "When the brain is exposed to anything random, like a slot machine or the shape of a cloud, it automatically imposes a pattern into the noise. But that isn't Snoopy, and you haven't found the secret pattern in the stock market." Instead, as author Jonah Lehrer writes more succinctly, "Your emotions have sabotaged common sense."

Flipping a coin ten times, people exhibit greater amazement at a streak of perfectly alternating heads and tails than at a random outcome, even though the odds of both are exactly the same. Likewise with a streak of ten consecutive heads, people often surmise, though incorrectly, "This coin is *due* for tails." Known as the "gambler's fallacy," this same misconception resulted in a Monte Carlo casino making millions of francs on gamblers who thought that a roulette wheel that landed on black twenty-six consecutive times must be ready to show a red. The dopamine in the room was likely palpable.

Finding these phantom patterns in things is not only natural but fun, along with the little high it elicits. For example, we can now prove that the popular children's hero Barney is the biblical Antichrist as laid out in the Book of Revelation's pronouncement of the "Beast's" number, 666. Barney is a CUTE PURPLE DINOSAUR. As the Romans substituted *V* for *U* we can do the same here: CVTE PVRPLE DINOSAVR. Extracting these Roman numerals leaves us with: CV VL DIV, and their Roman numeral equivalent: $100 + 5 + 5 + 50 + 500 + 1 + 5 = 666$. The odds are just too astonishing for this to be anything short of a *revelation*. (Feel that dopamine kick in.)

The world is just the size it is: 6,794,709,463 people and counting, as per the current—though now immediately out of date—"Population Clock." And we make it smaller. Ironically, with the prominence of the World Wide Web, our respective "worlds" have become even smaller yet. Instead of branching out and connecting with "random people in Madagascar," we become more and more sequestered in our own shrinking niches—'Tis a small world here in our Republican Knitting Group for Bird Lovers of North Carolina.

IF IGNORANCE IS BLISS THEN WHY AREN'T MORE PEOPLE HAPPY?

What event consistently causes groups of high school interviewees to anticipate experiencing the following feelings and emotions:

> Betrayal, Denial, Longing, Fear, Discomfort, Pain, Confusion, Anger, Nervousness, Sadness, Insecurity, and Loneliness?

It's not the death of a loved one. Not some violation of human rights, nor even the proposal to add an hour to the school day. This is a collection of high school students' responses to what they imagine they would feel were they led out into the blinding light from Plato's "Cave of False Reality" where they had lived their entire seventeen years.

The short story: Since the day you were born, you have lived in a cool, comfortable cave, chained down, watching shadows cast by a fire behind you. Given that these shadows are all you have ever known, they have become your reality. Yet at some point you are "led out" of the cave to experience the blinding light of the sun, shedding light on Reality. (Foreshadowing: The Latin roots of *educate* are "to lead out.") The new light hurts your eyes, and the new knowledge hurts your brain. But knowledge of Reality, Plato argues, is the highest good one can achieve.

Plato here gives us a motivation to overcome the alluring adage "Ignorance is bliss." While false notions may occasionally yield bliss, it is an unfounded bliss, and Plato clearly argues we should strive for something greater. In the popular movie *The Truman Show,* Truman is born into the false reality of a television set in which everyone in his life is an actor, as if the ultimate reality TV show. As the director of the show says at one point, "We accept the reality of the world with which we are presented." But viewers come to feel a real deficiency in Truman's life. Despite his situation being perfectly orchestrated for him—with a wife, a job, and even the weather finely tuned—we feel that his bliss is only superficial and we want something more for him. The real question is, do we want something more for ourselves?

Plato nicely anticipates what twenty-first-century neuroscience has empirically confirmed: We don't like to change our worldview. We don't even like it challenged. Imagine the upheaval of your own personal world were you to come out of a cave of your own, be it a new belief regarding Santa Claus, your complete reversal on political parties, or your realization that your new views on God were antithetical to what they've been all your life. Upon seeing support for the "other" side, you initially deny it and fight it (almost) to the death: "I don't care if it's impossible for one man to visit 6 billion people in one night, the presents are there!"

Then you feel confusion: "How *could* these presents end up in my house?" which typically couples with discomfort, thus creating a sense of fear—the fear of the unknown. As you overcome the pain and anger that results from the betrayal—betrayed by the mythical Santa Claus, your parents, or the playground at large—a sadness and longing start to take hold: You literally miss Santa and his watchful eye, even though you realize it was never there in the first place. Now you're alone again.

You can't undo the knowledge. This is part of the character building in one's accepting the quest to "see the light." You realize that you may discover things that you can't undo. As Lady Macbeth opines, "What's done cannot be undone." That psychic who seemed to talk to your deceased grandmother last year was just making things up—she employed simple tricks such as using vague statements, making lots of guesses, and even asking *you* questions versus telling you what she claimed to know. Now you can't go back into the cave, as you've acquired the curse of knowledge.

While you come to pity the cave dwellers you left behind, for they clearly don't have it right, you find a strange pang of envy—after all, they're blissful and have each other. When you return to lead them out they ridicule you, says Plato, and they have their own defense mechanisms in place: "We're just fine here, thank you." "No way are there these things you speak of *out there*." "Bright sun? No thanks." That is, if you can even speak to them—how can you possibly describe three dimensions to someone living in a world of two-dimensional shadows all their life?

So here we are now: Republicans and Democrats, atheists and theists, Santa Claus pushers and regular gift givers. What can we take from Plato? We must be open to the potential light sources out there, and realize that to see the truth by overcoming a false reality of our own requires a sincere quest that will be painful and lonely and scary at times. That we should not be deterred at the first sign of discomfort, for pain increases awareness. And from this journey that we can know that our foundations were earned. As the director in *The Truman Show* shares, "If he was absolutely determined to discover the truth, there's no way we could prevent him." And then, aptly, "Cue the sun!"

THE SELF

Being *Human* Is Not Just a Day Job

Author Salman Rushdie relates the consequences of the I'd-Rather-Be mentality through a tale of ancient Indian philosopher Chanakya. A disciple of Chanakya's questions the legitimacy of the claim that one can live in the world yet *not* live in the world simultaneously. In typical sagelike manner, Chanakya responds by giving the student a pitcher of water filled to the brim and instructs him to traverse the entire town's festival that day without spilling a drop, thus avoiding penalty of death. At the end of the day, after the student has successfully accomplished the task, Chanakya asks him to describe the day's festivities. Clearly, he knows nothing of them, having focused solely on the given task. Lesson learned. As the ancient Chinese proverb illuminates, "Teach me and I'll forget; show me and I may remember; involve me and I'll understand." The pitcher purportedly had a sticker that read, "I'd Rather Be . . . Participating in the Town's Festivities."

The correlation must be high between these bumper-sticker owners and those who take out their cell phones while at dinner to send text messages or answer a call while mid-conversation with a friend. Aside from doctors and parents awaiting calls from their respective patients, this now-popular antisocial social maneuver might as well come with its own little sticker—a phone sticker—that says, "I'd rather be talking to *this* guy." Add that to the self-inflicted live-time updates of Twitter and the Facebook phenomenon, and you have a perfect environment for the rebirth of the tragic hero of the Me Generation, Narcissus.

Christopher Lasch's 1979 bestseller, *The Culture of Narcissism,* brought to light the empty self-indulgence created by an information age. He believed that an overabundance of information actually resulted in a weaker sense of self and thus an incapacity to form meaningful relationships. You have to truly love yourself before you can love another. Worse yet, the bytes of information zipping around today make it seem like Lasch wrote of an age in which people communicated on the third-grade science class phones of two paper cups connected by a string. Facebook came around at just the right time, as psychologists noted a 30 percent increase in Americans' personality test scores for narcissism from 1982 to 2006. They couldn't have anticipated that in the "What is X doing now?" announcement section of X's Facebook page, when X types "Is getting married," that she was actually on her phone texting during the vows of her own wedding. You can also find such entries as ". . . is being robbed," and ". . . is late for work and can't find her keys." It's like people are creating *maps* of their lives instead of actual lives, akin to the vacationers who film the entire vacation to watch it later, so they can see the vacation that they had, while texting their friends about it all. But you're there *now.* You're with them right *now.* You can actually do it *now.*

The ever-elusive Now. Time flies when you're having fun. This "fun" often results from "living in the *now.*" Much of our internal angst derives from our constantly juggling what we coulda, woulda, shoulda done, with what could, would, should do, all the while, *doing:* driving a car at sixty miles per hour within inches of others doing the same ("Was I even driving just now?"). Fear results from anticipating something that might happen in the future, and anxiety as a result of what did happen in the past.

A major component of that arrow of time lies in our own view of it: When we're younger, time goes slower—progressing from age zero to one exactly doubles your day count. Versus when we're older, time passes more quickly—ahh, what's another year. And when consciously aware of time it can barely seem to pass at all. This psychological tidbit drives the adage "A watched toaster never toasts," as the watcher gives up because it simply takes too long. When unaware—such as when sleeping, or in the more enriching moments of being human such as when "in the zone" as an athlete, musician, or lover—time ceases to be a factor. And to further celebrate this concept of time, as Einstein showed in his Theory of Relativity, time is not even absolute or fixed. Instead it is relative to where one stands: The closer to the earth, the slower it goes—just think, your head is older than your feet.

Many cultures and worldviews avoid much of our "time angst" with different views of time. The Buddhist Wheel of Time treats time not as a straight arrow, but as something that circles back upon itself, creating a cycle of life, making it as difficult to pinpoint a "beginning" and an "end" as it would be to find those same points on a bike tire. Linguist Benjamin Whorf has us imagine how differently we would view our lives without our notions of past and future, with no interest in "exact sequences, dating, calendars, chronology," but instead with just the present. "Language shapes the way we think," he wrote, "and determines what we can think about." (He actually claimed the Aztecan Hopi people did live this way, though it turns out not to be the case—he just had trouble communicating with them, or the "no concept of time" report sold better than the "same as ours" one.) And, of course, we can't forget God, for whom, as Peter instructs us, "A day is like a thousand years, and a thousand years like a day." But this isn't really an option for us. Not "now" anyway.

So maybe that strangely aggressive, antagonistic response to this bumper-sticker wisdom can jolt us a bit:

> # I DON'T CARE WHAT YOU LOVE, WHAT YOUR OTHER CAR IS, OR WHAT YOU'D RATHER BE DOING

We can even change that other bumper-sticker command from "Hang Up and Drive" to "Hang Up and Live," start to get a little more control of time in our own lives, and keep from turning into that narcissus flower, because no one's got time for that.

If it's true that "All you need is love," then a brief survey of bumper stickers suggests that many Americans have all they need. Of course, philosophers and sages, poets and scientists throughout history have explored not just the value of love, but just what this love-stuff is anyway. If it's all we need, we should know what "it" is. We need more than the French non-definition definition, *je ne sais quoi,* or famed sex columnist *Sex and the City*'s Carrie Bradshaw's *zsa zsa zoo,* when in search of this life force.

French mathematician Blaise Pascal weighed in with his savvy insight "The heart has its reasons, of which reason is unaware." Thus the terms "*madly* in love," "infatuated," and "*crazy* about you" often describe the lover's relationship to the beloved. Basically, while passion may not be wholly rational, it has its reasons—so stop worrying and just go with it.

To avoid sounding like the desperate college boy using that day's philosophy class notes to woo a coed, the stoics intercede to put out the fire of all this passion-talk. The ancient Greek school of Stoicism flew the banner "Follow where reason leads." For them, passion not only caused, but was literally defined as, *suffering,* and the stoics held that to best achieve "the good," one should strive more for *apatheia*—peace of mind free from passion. Mind you, this approach has evolved over the years, with the current stoic seeming totally unemotional and closed off, apathetic to the rest of the world. The stoics of yore instead sought deeper ideals, couched in the four virtues: courage, justice, wisdom, temperance. They even discovered through their musings that we truly ought to love one another, as we are members of much greater communities than just our families and local village. As Socrates imparts, "I am not an Athenian or a Greek, but a citizen of the world."

From an evolutionary standpoint, yielding to the passions can certainly be defended. Nothing like a little evolution and biology to really get one's juices flowing. Various factors account for mate selection in humans. Pheromones—aka body odor—secretly provide cues to possible mates that help match immune systems that differ, thus allowing one parent to continue living in the case of the next bubonic plague. Physical symmetry also affects mate selection, at least on a subconscious level, as it seems to suggest greater health and ability to cope with varying environmental factors. Actress Cate Blanchett has earned the moniker of our species' "most symmetrical face," thus providing an objective explanation for all boyhood crushes.

Once contact has been made, the human chemical factories go into overdrive. The butterflies in the stomach, increased heart rate, and obsessive daydreaming about one's beloved all coincide with increased chemicals in the brain. While in the company of the prospective mate, one chemical cocktail heightens the senses, causing the feeling of euphoria. Immediately following intercourse, another cocktail—an aperitif or nice dessert wine may be a better metaphor—causes feelings of bonding and deeper connection. Thus, the "sex complicates things" observation is true, and for good reason: The so-called complication is that sex also creates babies, and two parents are much better than one when it comes to rearing offspring. Greater levels of bonding chemicals mean greater chances of lasting, happy relationships. No need to grind up and consume the loosely phallic rhinoceros horn believed by some to increase libido—it doesn't do anything other than harm the rhino and display one's ignorance. If you really need that added boost, recent studies show that consuming naturally grown Horny Goat Weed's heart-shaped leaves may soon replace taking the artificial drug Viagra, but they just need to re-name it first. And no need to order that extra drink at the bar—a depressant, alcohol actually has a negative effect on sex drive. Nature will whip up an aphrodisiac like none other once you lay eyes on a suitable mate.

So it turns out that the now popular heart symbol for love leads us astray. "I *brain* you," actually achieves greater accuracy, though is considerably harder to draw. To attain even greater precision, "I *lobe* you" narrows the focus on the specific part of the brain and sounds closer to our current adoration-laden vocabulary. Then again, the typical heart symbol looks nothing like the piece of meat it intends to represent, so maybe an oval with a line on the end could take its place—we don't want to lose the truth for the mere sake that "I *lobe* New York" doesn't feel right just yet. We'll get used to it.

Oftentimes, this reductionist account of love misses the point for many, or at the least serves as just one lens. The hopeful romantic cries, "There must be something more." Poets have tried to capture this—"My love for you is like a thousand oceans / Oceans like a thousand angels from above"—though even that seems to fall short. Philosopher Irving Singer suggests that Pascal was wrong in his suggestion that the heart is mysterious and unknown. Instead, he submits, love is an active and conscious process in which love for another manifests itself in the lover as a means by which that person shows "sheer gratuity." That love can literally change the lover by diminishing his or her trivial worldly desires, instead intensifying the almost magical act of bestowing. And the Buddha brings it all home: "Because we are not the result of any creator, we are all equal parts of an interconnected network. We integrate into this whole through love. This love provides . . . a harmony of the universe."

And all of this doesn't even touch on the various types of love as distinguished by the Greeks to better capture the various things that follow the heart symbol on bumper stickers (pizza, airplane noise, NY, etc.): *Eros:* passionate love (see aphrodisiacs above); *Agape:* pure love (see "magic of bestowing"); *Philia:* non-passionate love (such as that of friends); *Storge:* natural affection (of parents for children); *Xenia:* common love and hospitality.

Studies of monkeys show that lack of care and loving behavior toward them results in not only harmful psychological effects but physiological effects as well, and it has been suggested that intimacy and love serve a much greater role in the mental health of humans than nearly any other factor. As Singer writes, "The human species could survive without the art of the theater, or of painting, or of literature, or of music; but man would not be man without the art of mutual love." While we may need more than love, once we are nourished and fed, it seems like it—whatever it is—is a close second.

KISS: KEEP IT SIMPLE STUPID

Isaac Newton once remarked, "Nature is pleased with simplicity." And Nature is no dummy. So aside from the odd name-calling nature of this bumper-sticker wisdom, it may just be onto something.

Why do watches tick? That's a simple enough question for most of us in the Western world. But imagine a man in an aboriginal culture who finds a watch, like the man who encountered a magic Coke bottle in the movie *The Gods Must Be Crazy*. Having never seen a watch, he has no idea how its hands move in unison so precisely. So he posits that an invisible gremlin resides inside the watch doing all the work. After a few years transpire, a curious observer comes along and opens the back of the watch, exposing the gears that clearly cause the hands to tick. Mystery solved. But . . . our watch finder has become so emotionally and intellectually attached to his invisible friend that he posits the ticking of the watch as caused by both the gears *and* the gremlin. As Napoleon once quipped, "Give my watch to a savage, and he will think it has a soul." But we've come a long way since savagery.

The master of simplicity, medieval Franciscan friar William of Occam, explains how to go about choosing among competing theories, in our case here the Gears-*and*-Gremlin theory and the Gears-Only theory. First, determine if the two competing theories explain the given phenomenon equally well. If they do, then accept the simpler of the two, for the basic reason that it has a lesser likelihood of being wrong. With the principle termed "Occam's Razor," one can simply slice away the unnecessary part of a theory—in this case, the gremlin. The more moving parts needed to make a car run, the greater likelihood of a part breaking. Likewise with two equally powerful theories: the more "moving parts," the greater the chance it will break down.

"How does this relate to me?" one might ask, especially if one does not work in the fields of science, economics, or other areas where this regularly applies. Currently, two theories explain your own existence. You love, make moral decisions, and feel pain due to either (a) a physical body and immaterial invisible soul—a concept known as *dualism; or* (b) just a physical body—a concept known as *materialism.* It used to be the case that we were as ignorant about these things as our watch finder was about the mysterious ticking hands. But along came those curious observers (aka "scientists") who simply opened the back of the watch and discovered what was actually going on.

Neuroscientists have accomplished much for this venture in the past twenty years. They have opened the back of our watch—our skull—to reveal the inner working of the gears—our brain. Through the advent of recent scientific discoveries and techniques, we can pinpoint the exact physical and chemical pathways and locations in the brain and body of such human endeavors as experiencing pain, sadness and happiness, love, physical movement, sneezing, and making moral judgments.

So, all we need to do is return to our initial question: Do the two theories—dualism and materialism—explain our experience equally well? As it looks increasingly like they do, then the razor slices away the unnecessary invisible gremlin of dualism. But philosopher Thomas Nagel still argues they do not. He has us imagine what it is like to be a bat, suggesting that even the most imaginative person can only know what it is like for *that person* to be a bat, flying around at night, using sonar, eating mice, and sleeping upside down. No matter how much we know about bats and their brain function and social tendencies, we can never truly know what it is like for a *bat* to be a bat, because there's a subjective experience that a scientist cannot capture. Likewise with individual people. So, he concludes, this unknown "thing"—what is left over after all of the investigating—allows for, or *is*, the invisible soul.

In true marketplace-of-ideas fashion, philosopher Gilbert Ryle responds to what he calls "The dogma of the ghost in the machine." His concern does not involve science nor the subjective experience of what it's like to be something, but centers around language. Language has fooled us into assuming something false. For we often talk about the mind and soul in our daily lives—*mind your manners, he's got soul,* etc.—as though it is some*thing* that exists. But Ryle suggests we're just mixing up our categories in the same way we would if we claimed, "I have a left-handed glove, a right-handed glove, *and* a pair of gloves." *Pair* isn't something above and beyond the physical gloves, just as a mind or soul isn't something above and beyond the body and brain—they're just two ways of talking about the same physical thing. As Harvard psychologist Steven Pinker puts simply in *How the Mind Works,* "The mind is what the brain does."

Albert Einstein instructs us to "Make everything as simple as possible, but not simpler." That seems simple enough, and from someone hardly considered stupid. Maybe "Keep It Simple, *Smarty*" works better after all. Occam would be proud.

The KILL YOUR TELEVISION *Segment*

TELEVISION IS DRUGS

To give this the benefit of the doubt—for they surely can't mean this literally—think about the goal of television: selling advertising. The average thirty-second ad during prime time costs $122,000, though it runs upward of $700,000 for TV excellence such as *American Idol.* The longer they keep the viewers watching, the more they can charge advertisers. They know how to do this because they constantly view viewers—they scan their brains and monitor their hearts as subjects in laboratories view various images, color combinations, and themes. As the CEO of CBS shared in 1997, "We're here to serve advertisers. That's our *raison d'être.*" This is why they tell you about the winner of the next round *after* this "word" from "our sponsors." A word, hardly. You spend over a quarter of your viewing time watching commercials. And if you're watching that American phenomenon the Super Bowl, in the four-hour event you see a total of about twelve minutes of football. So, if by "drug" you mean something like the dictionary definition—"causes addiction, habituation, or a marked change in consciousness, typically in a deleterious manner"—then television is certainly drug-*like.*

So is the solution to BLOW UP YOUR TV? Probably so, if you agree that EVERYTHING I LEARNED I LEARNED FROM TV. If that's the case, then you've likely come to think to yourself, TELEVISION RUINED MY LIFE. A fair conclusion if you're anywhere near the "average" person watching twenty-eight hours of television each week, or even half that, really. Geez, all those sixty-five-year-olds have spent a full nine of their years mesmerized by good old-fashioned propaganda. Along with the twenty-one years spent sleeping, at least we're getting some answer to the nostalgic "Where'd the time go?"

Growing up watching all that television, you likely had few opportunities to **FIGHT PRIME TIME: READ A BOOK** (preferably this one). And if you were like most twelve-year-olds, then you could name more brands of beer than you could U.S. presidents. If only you had read those books instead, you'd have at least been free to **QUESTION TELEVISION** and then **KILL YOUR TV BEFORE IT KILLS YOUR BRAIN.** As Aldous Huxley warned in *Brave New World,* we have an "almost infinite appetite for distractions"—we are *Amusing Ourselves to Death,* as the title of Neil Postman's book suggests. But once you become aware of all this, you can **REJECT MIND CONTROL: TURN OFF YOUR TV.** After all, **WHY DO YOU THINK THEY CALL IT PROGRAMMING?** 📺 anyway? So, **TURN OFF TV, TURN ON LIFE.** Because, as I saw on a bumper sticker somewhere, **IF EVERYONE DEMANDED PEACE INSTEAD OF ANOTHER TELEVISION SET THERE'D BE PEACE. —JOHN LENNON.**

THE MORE THINGS CHANGE THE MORE THEY STAY THE SAME

This popular French proverb provides a great example of paradox. While the statement seems inherently contradictory, it also imparts deeper wisdom. On the one hand, if something constantly maintains a certain quality—i.e., ever-changing—the thing stays the same, in that one respect at least. Yet in this bumper-sticker wisdom, the consistent quality maintained is "change"—*not* staying the same—and thus it reminds us of the impermanence inherent in life. Things change, and *that's* something that will always be the same. And on a deeper level, change may not steer us as far from the status quo as we might imagine, and thus what endures through the change deserves more of our attention.

This interplay between sameness and change plays a key role in philosophical discussions of "Personal Identity," thus informing such topics as cloning, stem-cell research, animal rights, mortality, and artificial intelligence, as well as addressing just what it means to be an authentic person—or, as occasional once-friends criticize past-friends as "having become a *different* person." Much of one's identity intertwines with the name of that person, and so this practice of naming requires further investigation.

In a favorite thought experiment reported by Plutarch, circa A.D. 100, the ship of Theseus changed so drastically over time that, eventually, none of the parts from the original ship remained, and the original parts were all stored in a warehouse. When asked, "Which is the true Theseus's Ship?" respondents typically split down the middle, half choosing the ship floating in the water with no original parts, and half choosing the reassembled collection of dilapidated original parts in the warehouse. The ancient Greek philosopher Heraclitus frames this problem fluidly: "You cannot step in the same river twice." Over time, nothing about a particular river is the same—its path changes, the embankments erode and re-form, it acquires water from different sources, and the actual water molecules remain in constant flux. Yet, we still call it the *same* river.

Clearly the name of something isn't that thing at all. It has very little to do with that thing and serves more as a convenience and a placeholder than anything else. In the words of a Buddhist dialogue, a name is "Only a way of counting, a term, a label, a convenient designation." Because things change. Musical groups change (every single member in some cases). Sports teams change—as comedian Jerry Seinfeld muses: "Because the players are always changing [teams] . . . you're actually rooting for the clothes . . . You are standing and cheering and yelling for your clothes to beat the clothes from another city." And people change, drastically, over an average span of 81.3 years.

The irrelevance of a name and its participation in any sort of deeper reality is likely blocked by the psychological connection we develop with names. They come to truly mean something. Brand names such as Coca-Cola stand for much more than a drink, as do many others that have been marketed "successfully." Names of loved ones instill feelings of past experiences that have touched us. And our own names elicit a deeply profound meaning, as is evidenced by our reaction when we meet another of our namesake, or by our childhood response to the bullies who twisted our name to tease us on the playground. Setting aside emotion, when we look for the *true* object—the real person—we realize that the name is no longer relevant. We have changed our lens and are no longer concerned with convenience. In saying, "That *is* the same guy I met last week," Bill Clinton's infamous "It depends on what the meaning of the word *is* is" comes to mind; we realize that he was truly waxing philosophical in his defense of certain "affairs" that took place in the White House.

It turns out that we do use "same" and "is" in two different ways. If you have the "same" car as the one advertised on television, you have the same *type* of car, though if you and your roommate share the same car, then you share the same *token* car. It is this token sense of "same" that interests us concerning people. When we investigate whether Jim is the *same* person we once knew, we don't want "same type" but "same token." Thus, the futuristic thought experiment provides some difficulty: If we eventually download Joan's consciousness onto a computer and then, upon her death, clone her and reinsert her consciousness, is that the *same* person (i.e., token) or just someone very similar (i.e., type)? Clearly, we hope for the former in our eventually achieving some sort of immortality, for what use would it be if "I" die and then someone else lives on? Ditto for all afterlife scenarios.

Maybe it's true that nothing stays the "same" in the deep sense and that it really is a matter of convenience. While this may not satisfy us psychologically, at the least it provides one more glimpse into the depths of our own psyche, the world, and our place in it. It turns out that when presidential candidate Barack Obama ran for office in 2008 on a platform based on "Change" that he might as well have based it on "Same," though the bumper stickers wouldn't have sold as well.

CACCA OCCURRETH

This is pseudo-fancy-speak for that infamously popular bumper sticker "*C'est la Vie*," though knowing that *Forrest Gump* earned a rating of PG-13, we can delve further. In the movie, the now-famous Forrest is running cross-country and a stranger approaches him: "I'm in the bumper-sticker business and I've been trying to think of a good slogan and . . . I thought you might be able to help me . . . Whoa! Man, you just ran through a big pile of dog shit!"

"It happens," Forrest responds.

SHIT HAPPENS

This deeply philosophical doctrine has a smelly foot in two seemingly antithetical camps: the East and the West. Both can help shed some light on bumper-sticker wisdom . . . or maybe the bumper-sticker wisdom sheds some light on them.

A basic tenet of Buddhism involves the relinquishing of desire and letting go of what one holds most dear. In this way, we become a part of the Oneness of the universe—the cosmic dance known as karma in which everything dynamically interconnects. Zen Master Suzuki Roshi helps us understand this as if we were the water in a pond before birth: At birth the confused Easterner sees himself as a droplet in a waterfall—separate and fearful. But upon death he returns to the river below and feels one with it again. "How very glad the water must be to come back to the original river!" Roshi concludes, urging us to realize this during our current plot, as "Our life and death are the same thing."

That said, whether you're fired from your job, find that red sock leaking into your load of whites, or step in poop, it's all One. If you're truly connected to the Oneness of the universe then there's nothing to curse or fear. Shit just happens.

The Western approach is slightly less poetic, though equally beautiful. It requires that we squelch our natural inclination to assign meaning and patterns to meaningless phenomena. No need to constantly ask, "Why did that happen?" whether it be good or bad. *Scientific American* columnist Michael Shermer writes, "Our brains are belief engines: evolved pattern recognition machines that connect the dots and create meaning out of the patterns that we think we see in nature." While a fun exercise—such as turning collections of stars into animals or finding religious faces on toast—it often leads us astray from what's really going on: nothing. And when nothing's going on, then shit can just happen and there is no need to try to decode what the universe is "telling" you, what supernatural beings have in store for you, if everything happens for a reason and you just need to play detective, or if it was "in the stars." Good things happen and bad things happen. Coincidences Happen.

But we love to play the "No Coincidences Game," as when we assign meaning to dreams as though they forecast otherwise chance encounters. In a thirty-year span, we dream about people over ten thousand times. Yet, when a long-lost friend calls the day after we've dreamt of them flying through the air, we assign meaning to that. "What are the odds?" we exclaim as we revel in our psychic moment. But this is not a question to be taken lightly—given the number of opportunities, we should *expect* this to happen. Shit happens, good and bad. And what about the 9,999 people who didn't call? We conveniently forget about those because, what's there to remember, nothing? Shit happens again. On top of all of this, with a world of dreamers running the same nightly experiments, we should *expect* some of the dreamees to call the next day, even with odds as low as one in a billion.

We also love to play the "Meaning Game," and it's fun. But we're terrible with randomness and we hate it. For this reason Apple had to change their purely random "Shuffle" function on the iPod to "non-random but *seems* random"—people weren't happy with hearing Britney Spears three consecutive times even though we should expect this over a long randomized sample. We're just bad at doing the math behind really big numbers. So when the TV psychic tells the audience to get a coin and flip it ten times guaranteeing a run of ten straight heads, he only needs an audience of 1,024. Yet those who succeed feel like they're the Chosen One: "Why me? No coincidence here." They'll probably pay the psychic some of their hard-earned money because of it.

But things happen. Some we call "good" and some "bad." That's what things *do*. They occur. So we can go completely PG, conjugate Forrest's response, and acquire even more accuracy with greater simplicity: **IT HAPPENED.**

GOT SOUL?

It depends what you mean by "soul." Seriously. When you ask someone who answers this question in the affirmative just what this thing is that they've *got*, you often get a response along the lines of "I dunno." Then, following a pause, they typically give you the ol' switch-a-roo, "I mean, *you* know." When pressed further— "But I don't know. I have no idea. It's *your* thingamajig"—the answer often resembles something more like poetic metaphor than any *thing* they've actually *got*.

So if by "soul" you mean "Lots of gumption and a funky, authentic way of sharing the human condition," then yes, just go to the local blues bar and wait for the band to start. Lots of that *soul* there. Or if you mean the term for *mates* who get along just splendidly, always laughing at the same jokes, supporting each other, and sharing their lives together, then yes, there are "soul mates."

And if you mean something more like the idea of an "essence," just like cars have, or an orange peel, or any other being or object, then yes, your car's got soul. We know what you mean.

But an affirmative answer to this bumper-sticker question is not substantiated if it refers to something like "an invisible thing that flies out of your nose when you sneeze," as Pope Gregory III and many religious did leading up to the Age of Enlightenment. While that was somewhat of an improvement on the devil-flying-into-you theory of sneezing also popular at the time, Gregory implemented the "God Bless You" to prevent a potentially soulless sneezer from catching the bubonic plague. And it works—just try it the next time someone sneezes and see if they get the plague, or swine flu even. Though in our current politically correct climate, it's strange that only the sneezer gets blessed: Why not change the zeitgeist of sneezing and bless everyone?

Nor can a "yes" response mean "Thing that allows us to love," much like Plato did, as best paraphrased by Owen Wilson in *Wedding Crashers*: "True love is your soul's recognition of its counterpoint in another"—and he claims he read it on a bumper sticker. It turns out that you don't need to invent ghost stories to fall in love. Our bodies help us do this through the use of nature's perfume, pheromones. And those feelings of butterflies we feel when our beloved calls, or the attachment we experience after being intimate, results from our bodies' chemicals—great for getting people together and keeping them together so they can mate and raise offspring of our species. And when the mating happens, oh, just wait for the hormones to kick in. No ghosts needed in the romantic endeavor.

We just need to think about it for a moment, and not in the "I believe because it's absurd" pseudo-thinking offered by Christian theologian Tertullian, but from a place of empathy. It's certainly an understandable starting point for our comprehending the world. Long before the Age of Enlightenment, when your caveman buddy died and you burned the inert body, with no explanation for such a turn of events, a "spirit" rising into the sky toward a peaceful place seems as good a guess as any. Prehistoric cultures nearly universally buried their dead with artifacts they would need on their next adventure. But with all we now know (i.e., *Enlightenment*) it's somewhat of a surprise that this continues, as evidenced by, among myriad other things, the $122 iPhone replica made of *paper* for those in China who believe that whatever is burned with a body after death can be used in the afterlife. Maybe we'll finally get a call from one of these phone users and get proof of the afterlife—or maybe we won't, and this will instead be proof that the undead didn't burn a copy of the correct calling plan to take with them.

But if this soul-thing has no more use in today's culture, why keep shoving the phantom peg into a round hole? But even if Einstein was right when he wrote "The concept of a soul without a body seems to me empty and devoid of meaning," go ahead and keep using the term—we think we know what you mean.

READING IS SEXY

This bumper-sticker wisdom really preaches to the converted with this self-selecting demographic. While "sexy" clearly involves some apples-to-oranges-style value judgments—for you may disagree as to whether Justin Timberlake is "bringing sexy back"—it's worth seeking a foundation for sexiness. Of course, one must consider the content of the reading. Reading up on how to eat roadkill: not sexy. Reading about the deeper meaning behind bumper stickers and thus an intrinsic connection with one's self and their intimate bond to those around them: sexy. Ironically, reading about gametes and the fertilization process and development of chromosomes through sexual reproduction: not that sexy. But reading about the locked eyes of two impassioned lovers in gentle embrace on a cool summer evening leading up to all of the "gamete stuff": sexy.

Surveying the dictionary definitions of "sexy" and their relation to the act of reading will help to further our investigation.

1. *Tending to arouse sexual desire or interest.* Freud suggests that much of our sexuality hibernates in our subconscious. The more we come to know ourselves and bring to the surface what our superego suppresses, the more we avoid our ego's defense mechanisms and tap into our libido. Reading plays an instrumental role in such deep introspection. That's pretty sexy.

2. *(Slang) Highly appealing, interesting.* You're the one choosing the books for the likely reason exactly stated in this definition. Sexy, as charged.

3. *Provoking.* Given that you're reading someone else's book, with ideas not your own, reading is by definition provoking. And if you're reading your own book (aside from copyediting), get over yourself and go get sexy.

4. *Naughty.* Isn't it at least just a little naughty, getting into the mind of someone else who's sharing their fantasies, stories, thoughts, and discoveries? Readers can be such naughty voyeurs.

5. *Lively.* Reading actually burns calories, especially if you read books that make you laugh, cry, or pound your fist. In contrast to the non-lively, unsexy "couch potato," readers can avoid couches and read under trees, in cafés sipping tea, or nuzzled up in bed with a lover. Additionally, maintaining an active brain has been proven to ward off Alzheimer's disease—in the *use it or lose it* mentality of a muscle, reading is like a lively little weight room for the brain. How lively. How sexy.

So keep reading. You're only getting sexier by the page.

VALUES
What's It Worth to Ya?

BOTTLED WATER IS FOR SUCKERS

Nowhere in history does the phrase "Selling ice to Eskimos" apply more aptly than to the bottled-water fiasco. And not just because the analogue to ice in this case is its melted counterpart. We Eskimos have been duped.

"There's gold in them thar hills," came the cry in the 1980s. "Blue gold!"

"Wait. You're going to put dirtier, less palatable water in a bottle and ship it around the world to sell," pausing between sips of tap water, "to people who already get it for *free?*"

"If they're willing to spend billions of dollars each year on phone psychics, this will be even easier. We'll even name our first bottling Naïve. Or maybe we should spell it backward just to slip it by the consumer, take the weird little dots off the *i*. Evian still has a nice ring to it. We'll put a picture of a mountain on it."

If this week in America is like the week before, and the week before that, then we drank a billion bottles of water, and will drink another billion next week. In a time of great financial struggle and concern for our planet's survival, this life force must be cleaner and better tasting . . . right?

Most blind taste tests actually show the palatability of tap water. This should be of no surprise, as tap water is more highly regulated. Even in our more highbrow case of wine tasting, expert oenophiles—fancy name for "wine snobs"—are easily tricked into thinking a white wine with red food coloring is actually red wine, or that wine from a "$90" bottle tastes better than the *same* wine in a bottle with "$10" on it. Okay, so humans are gullible. They form preconceived notions. What's the harm?

For you, the consumer, the only harms are your drinking a less-regulated product at greater cost. For you, the environment, the only harms are the massive fuel and emissions required to ship this heavy substance around the world, and all the bottles left to deal with. For you, one of the billion who don't have access to safe drinking water, you're probably not reading this book.

To further illustrate, Princeton University ethicist Peter Singer uses the concept of a "Global Village." He suggests that we have a moral duty to all the members of our village, even if we don't see them, and especially if we can do so without "sacrificing anything of comparable moral importance," as in his clear-cut example in which we should muddy our pants if it saves the life of a drowning child.

A quick trip to Fiji provides a perfect application. Due to the country's isolation and volcanic soil, much of their population cannot get safe drinking water. The Fiji Company boasts of this on their website: "Fiji is far away. But when it comes to drinking water, 'remote' happens to be very, very good." So they paint a hibiscus flower on every bottle and ship it ten thousand miles to San Francisco, where someone sits in a bath of perfectly safe drinking water straight from the springs of Yosemite, sipping Fiji. Little does our bather know, there is likely more fecal matter in the bottle than in the tub. Fiji water has three times the colony-forming units for E. coli—the bacteria found in human feces—than the "recommended maximum." As other bumper-sticker wisdom reminds us "Shit Happens," but who'da' thunk it happens in our now-strangely-nutty-tasting "premium" bottled water?

So, in light of the thousands in our global village who die daily from diseases transmitted through contaminated water, Singer suggests we instead "Put that dollar in a jar . . . carry a water bottle . . . send all the money to . . . someone who has real needs. And you're no worse off."

Funny, in that not-so-funny way, that we'll drive ten minutes out of our way to buy fifteen gallons of gas for twenty cents cheaper per gallon and then walk in the Gas Mart and plunk down three dollars for something we get for free. Sucker.

ART IS EVERYWHERE

Well, yes and no. Yes if you mean, "Who are you to tell me that this blank canvas isn't *art*?" No if you want "art" to mean anything: If everything is art, then nothing is art. Imagine finding the entry in the dictionary:

Art *n*. \ärt\: 1. Everything. 2. Anything. 3. Whatever.

Philosophers, not surprisingly, have spilled some ink on the question "What is art?" Post-modernism, for starters, provides an answer just one small step removed from the parody definition above, basically holding that art is whatever one thinks is art. At least here we have a criterion: Someone at some point has to have considered something as art. This likely leaves us wanting more. As we walk into a room to see a pencil lying on the floor, we have to survey billions of people to see if anyone considers it art before we deem it not so.

Intent-based theories push us one step further to answering the question—that it is not the *viewer's* discretion but that of the *creator*. If someone creates something with the intention of creating art, then it is art. As for our cockeyed pencil, we just need to discover if someone has intended it as art and declared it so. Our opinion plays no role here.

Author and philosopher Leo Tolstoy gives us something deeper in his aptly titled "What Is Art?": *infectiousness*. He suggests that true art requires that spectators are "infected by the feelings which the author has felt." This likely brings us closer to what we want from a classification of art, though we must be concerned if we don't feel the *joy* Beethoven intended in his *Ode to Joy* and thus declare it "counterfeit art."

Now that we have made this topic perfectly obscure, we come to an even more pressing question, "What is *good* art?" This is a Picasso of another color. As a matter of pragmatics (and politics), the U.S. government's National Endowment for the Arts (NEA) claims to answer this. Under the banner "A great country deserves great art," one of their missions is "supporting works of artistic excellence." In 2008, they had a budget of over $140 million to accomplish this mission. The issue of "good" art definitely came into question in the past when they awarded grants to the likes of Andres Serrano for his *Piss Christ* (a jar of urine containing a plastic crucifix) and Robert Mapplethorpe's collection of erotic photos.

Plato once wrote, "It is impossible to understand the science of shoes until one understands what science is." While an apt quote for our creationist-"science" proponents, it also highlights the difficulty in assigning value to an already slippery concept. Does *good* art relate to the skill needed to create it? Although nearly every beginning guitarist can play most Green Day songs, the band has still earned the moniker of goodness. And art icon Andy Warhol's *Red Disaster* poses no challenge for the artistic neophyte: a canvas of pure red. Not much of a disaster for him as it currently hangs in Boston's Museum of Fine Arts (emphasis on *Fine*). Likewise, not all art that is difficult to make is necessarily good. So does good art involve popularity? Was Picasso's *Garçon à la Pipe good* because it sold for over $100 million at a recent auction? Is Neil Diamond *better* than Green Day *just because* he's sold more records? But Van Gogh didn't sell a single of his nine hundred paintings in his lifetime. It would seem odd to claim that he wasn't good then, but is now. Better off dead, maybe.

This topic admittedly involves as many (if not more) questions than it has answers. Part of the *art* of philosophy, maybe. But answers exist in this realm, and the unrequited questions can maybe illuminate the very *je ne sais quoi* of art that makes it so powerful in the first place.

ABSTINENCE: 100% EFFECTIVE

This is the corollary of that sports adage "You don't make 100 percent of the shots you don't take." Though in the case of this bumper-sticker wisdom, that's exactly the point: not making the shot. In our nonsporting application with this bumper sticker, most people most of the time just want to play the game, take a few shots, and after they've flung the "ball" toward the basket, happily walk away midflight assuming—hoping, even—that it didn't go in. Kids start practicing by themselves early on, often imagining what it might be like to be on such a team. And if you don't practice at all, Nature sneaks up on you while you're sleeping and forces you to play. It's like our *bodies* want us to have sex whether *we* want to or not.

The clear conflict of interest notwithstanding, recent studies show that in addition to all the other benefits of sex—endorphins, immunity, heightened senses, smiling a lot, etc.—increasing the rate of intercourse from two times per week to three slows the aging process, not only resulting in a more youthful appearance but also adding three years to one's life. So you can throw away all those cosmetic creams and magic milkshakes and embrace the "Make Love, Not War" bumper-sticker wisdom. It's like our bodies have cast their vote on the answer to the purpose-of-life question: Have sex and procreate.

This bumper-sticker wisdom is true, with one exception: all of the purported virgin births. Stories like these occur more often than many realize. Mary's virgin birth came at a time in history when many other, oddly similar myths abounded, including the virgin births of both Krishna and Genghis Khan; Horus, born to the virgin Isis; Mercury; Romulus; and many others. Fortunately for all those early writers, they predated copyright laws and plagiarism taboos. Though part of the mystery of Mary's event emerges when we realize that the prophecy referenced in the Bible used the Hebrew word for "young woman" (*almah*) and was mistranslated as "virgin"—understandably, "Young Woman Birth" isn't much around which to build a religion.

A better bumper sticker might read, "Abstinence: The best chance to give birth to a supernatural being." Though it turns out that various species commonly experience virgin birth—known as parthenogenesis from the Greek *parthenos* (virgin) and *genesis* (creation)—such as various wasps, fish, and Komodo dragons. We might imagine a *Far Side* cartoon featuring amoebas that would hold as divine two amoebas who, many years ago, had actual sexual intercourse to produce an offspring instead of their asexual reproduction.

Virgin births aside, abstaining from sex clearly prevents pregnancy, which for some can be a very viable life choice. Buddhism teaches that one should avoid any attachment to all non-permanent things, including attachment to humans. In this way one can avoid obstacles blocking the path to Nirvana—the total peace of mind gained from connection to the Oneness, the permanence, of the universe. With the extremes of the Buddhist and benefits-of-sex approaches in place, this might provide a good opportunity to apply Aristotle's Doctrine of the Mean, as summarized by Greek Philosopher Thales, "All things in moderation." Or not.

But this bumper sticker alludes to abstinence-*only* education, providing a great example of theory versus practice. In *theory*, it should suffice to tell a thirteen-year-old, "Don't have sex. It could result in children and shatter all of your dreams or you could contract an STD and your genitals will fall off." Unfortunately, in *practice*, this doesn't work. Studies show that abstinence-only programs have a considerably greater failure rate when compared with programs that also include sex education and information on contraception. Ironically, they can even lead to an *increase* in pregnancies.

Some programs have encouraged teenagers to sign "virginity pledges" that, while slightly delaying the average age of the first sexual experience, result in initiates who eventually have sex at the same rate as non-initiates yet are much more likely to avoid using birth control when they do eventually break that pledge they made when thirteen.

Abstinence-only education is like telling a fifteen-year-old he should wait until twenty-one to drink alcohol, but that if he ever does get drunk, he can just drive himself home. Unfortunately, this is just what the Catholic Church has done. On the Pope's recent visit to Africa—where HIV/AIDS is more deadly than on any other continent and where most infections spread through sexual intercourse—he admonished them that AIDS "cannot be overcome by the distribution of condoms." As Catholic doctrine clearly denotes, *all* contraception is bad: "Every sperm is sacred," sing the boys from Monty Python, "Every sperm is good." Despite the World Health Organization's warning of a global pandemic that has already killed over 20 million people and their urging that condoms must be distributed, the president of the Pontifical Council for the Family, Cardinal Alfonso Trujillo, instead misinformed his congregation that condoms contain microscopic holes in them, rendering them useless. Author Christopher Hitchens finds it hard to imagine anyone else with more "authority to inflict the greatest possible suffering in the least number of words." Though with the recent mass sexual delinquency of Catholic priests and its cover-up by those in charge, sex education seems like something they should abstain from.

It turns out that the hard data—*practice*—does not support abstinence-only education—*theory*. The result of putting a Pandora's box out for kids, instructing them that whatever they do they should not look inside, was correctly anticipated by the Greek storytellers. Curiosity killed the cat, and, as philosopher Thomas Hobbes once wrote, is the "lust of the mind." But it doesn't have to kill us—we just need to be better coached on how to play the game.

BABY ON BOARD!

Typically displayed as warnings hanging from car windows in the form of a yellow diamond, they also exist in bumper-sticker format. And even if you put a "bumper sticker" on your wall at home, it doesn't morph into a "wall sticker," so we can address the bumper-sticker-style window ornament here.

They became popular after a company began producing them in 1984 "to improve driver awareness and child safety." If you're like most drivers, you have never collided with a baby-warning-bearing vehicle—clear proof that they're doing their job. The assumption is that, as your car is spinning out of control, your soymilk latte spilling on your cashmere sweater, you will avoid the warning-bearing car and instead drive your car into the baby-free victim. Another baby saved. It also assumes that these warning signs correctly denote what they say, and are not left dangling in the car even while the driver merely cruises the strip with friends. And if one sees a parked car on a hot day with this decal on display, should they look to see that the baby is okay?

These signs suffer the similar fate of the now-illegal rearview-mirror-hanging conspiracy of protection offered by Native American dreamcatchers, crucifixes, and lucky fuzzy dice. We hang these things in our car for a (false) sense of security: Nothing bad could happen if I have captured good dreams, gods watching, Lady Luck in the house, or a Baby on Board. But instead, just like those who bathe in magic water instead of taking that prescription and getting some rest, these things serve to obscure our already imperfect vision, resulting in more accidents than they prevent. It's like installing an additional blind spot. And with the parody stickers— "Baby Driving," "Baby I'm Bored," "Mother-in-Law in Trunk"— now outnumbering this bumper-sticker wisdom five to one, the theory of causation versus prevention gains even more clout.

Much of this derives from the human inclination that doing *something* supersedes doing *nothing,* even if the "something" yields a worse result—what psychologists refer to as "action bias." It turns out that the negative feelings of *doing nothing and failing* override the diminished sense of failure upon having actually acted even if the action yields less success. We'd rather fail but say, "At least I tried," than refrain from acting and have a better chance at success. In stock trading, for example, it is often better to hold a stock long term (i.e., non-action), but stockbrokers appear better in their clients' eyes if they act because, after all, clients aren't paying them to do nothing.

So at least we can understand the need to *do something* and hang that added blind spot. Though given the whole "all humans created equal" thing we could all just assume the "Human on Board!" warning sign and have no need to hang it at all. Then we can crash into others in a more non-discriminatory manner.

FEMINISM IS THE RADICAL NOTION THAT WOMEN ARE PEOPLE

This bumper sticker provides the added bonus of affording an opportunity for distilling rhetoric. As you—the clearly advanced reader—know, it is couched in the term "radical." The only problem is, places still exist in the world where this rhetoric is wasted, or worse, where it is taken literally. Places like Saudi Arabia where women can be jailed for being raped, or in Africa, Britain, Norway, and many others where an estimated 120 million young girls undergo genital mutilation or the less dramatic but all too real discrimination in academia in which scientific hiring proposals are granted in disproportionate numbers to men when gender-specific names appear.

Many institutions do not afford women opportunities equal to those of men. The Catholic Church, for one, has divided the masculine and the feminine. As Christ was a man, only men can hold the highest-ranking positions such as priests, bishops, and cardinals, and women are forbidden from ever holding such ranks. In a sense, the male priests are married to the feminine "church" (i.e., "her"). Since women can't marry women, the catechism of the church doubly forbids them from ever holding such an esteemed rank in the first place. Those studying to become sacred ministers in the church are required by church law to study the works of a saint, Thomas Aquinas, who wrote that women are "defective" and "misbegotten."

More recently, renowned theologian and founder of Lutheranism, Martin Luther, shared additional insights, noting that "Girls begin to talk and to stand on their feet sooner than boys because weeds always grow up more quickly than good crops." And lastly, popular Republican pundit and self-proclaimed "voice of God" Rush Limbaugh enlightens us by suggesting that "Feminism was established to allow unattractive women access to mainstream society." He goes on to reference them as "feminazis," as if the seeking of gender equity in any way relates to the horrors of Nazi Germany.

Feminism as a movement has shot itself in the foot somewhat, likely in an attempt to overcompensate for past injustices hoping to land right on target. UCLA feminist Sandra Harding argues that Isaac Newton's *Principia Mathematica* is a "rape manual" as "science is a male rape of female nature." And Susan McClary explains how Beethoven's Ninth—"one of the most horrifying moments in music"—depicts the "throttling murderous rage of a rapist incapable of attaining release." Through this lens, one could imagine a feminist critique for the repeated use of the phallic *i* symbol here.

Before we throw the ceiling out with the glass, we should first look at just what is being said. As with most cause-and-effect discussions, it often distills down to the ol' nature/nurture controversy. The question is, what causes the variation between men and women?

On the nurture side we have the often off-putting "gender feminists." Their general response to the idea of biological, innate differences among men and women? "Poppycock," Bella Abzug retorts. Gender feminists instead argue that men and women differ due to social factors such as upbringing and cultural influence. Yet science divulges the exact opposite in support of the nature side: the "equity feminist" camp. The "fuel" used to create boys as fetuses—androgens, including testosterone—causes very different outcomes from the "fuel" that creates females—estrogens. Thus, sex differences are universal and not unique to just Western culture, and men develop larger brains with more neurons while women have a higher percentage of gray matter. It even turns out that Americans do not treat their sons and daughters differently in any important manner. As the vocational tests show, the two sexes simply have different interests, with men interested in "realistic" and "theoretical" activities, and women in "artistic" and "social" endeavors. It's no wonder they each succeed at tasks of different sorts.

All of this is of great interest, obviously, especially if one is writing a book to match sexes with which planet they would hail from. But of interest here is the ethical claim made by our bumper-sticker wisdom. "Different" doesn't necessarily mean better or worse, even if those in power tell you it does. And even if a representative seems like he or she is from another planet, their rights remain intact. So what if men and women generally enjoy different movies—women having evolved the propensity to emote and relish a "chick flick" (first time this phrase has been used in an article supporting feminism) and men to enjoy their "guy cry" (Wikipedia it)? So what if one group, on average, jumps higher or lifts more weight than the other? Differences *do* exist among the sexes from Day One, though no single difference affords rights to one group over the other. To see things any other way would seem pretty radical.

HOW CAN SOMEONE BE PRO-LIFE IF THEY ARE PRO-WAR?

The question certainly gives the appearance that the questioner actually does know the respondent's answer, and that the answer contradicts itself. A conceivable response to this accusation could rely on the innocence of the respective victims: Fetuses are innocent and evil tyrants deserve what's coming to them. More important, war prevents the death of other innocent citizens.

This bumper-sticker wisdom of the "Tactful Finger Pointer" here exists in a more overt, uncouth form:

> ## HOW CAN SOMEONE BE "PRO-LIFE," PRO-DEATH PENALTY, PRO-GREED, PRO-WAR? . . . STOP BEING A HYPOCRI†E.

The questioning (i.e., accusing) of our "Uncouth Finger Pointer" here—who probably doesn't get invited back to Easter brunch very often—requires a little more work. The scare quotes around "Pro-life" provide a nice starting place, because war and the death penalty clearly do not seem "Pro-life"; nor do they appear very Christian.

Figuring out the Bible's stance on the death penalty is a bit like pinning Jell-O to a tree. In Genesis, God forbids the killing of Cain even after Cain kills his brother Abel: He puts a mark on Cain's head and notes, in a strangely aggressive manner, "Whosoever slayeth Cain, vengeance shall be taken on him sevenfold." Multiplying "slaying" by seven without actually killing the person poses an interesting intellectual challenge, but the "don't kill" message is clear. Yet throughout the rest of the Old Testament we find numerous crimes punishable by stoning to death, impalement, or burning to death, such as working on Saturday (e.g., a man who gathered some wood one Saturday afternoon) or looking back at a city during its destruction (e.g., Lot's wife—to add salt to the wound, she was turned into a pillar of salt). We read an interesting twist of biblical law in Deuteronomy, in which rape is punishable by death if the woman is engaged, but if she is single then the rapist earns the sentence of being married to his victim (and he has to give her dad fifty shekels of silver). Yet, with all of this, in

Leviticus we read, "You shall not take vengeance, nor bear any grudge, but you shall love your neighbor as yourself."

The New Testament offers a slightly more forgiving approach as we get Jesus' affable "Whoever slaps you on your right cheek, turn the other to him also." Yet this same "newer" testament has Jesus affirming the Mosaic law that for one who fails to honor his mom and dad, "let him be put to death." Humph.

As for the "pro-war" concern, St. Thomas Aquinas and other major church figures adhere to Just War Theory, justifying war when certain criteria are met. And the church did support the Crusades in the Middle Ages in an attempt to take back the Holy Land from Muslim rule. Yet it is truly difficult to imagine a soldier holding in his heart Jesus' command to "love your enemies" while killing them and causing other "collateral damage." A vision of Monty Python's "Holy Hand Grenade" comes to mind as the high priest blesses the device commanding it to "Blow thine enemy to tiny bits." An accidentally leaked Intelligence Update from Secretary of Defense Dick Cheney showed numerous cover pages depicting U.S. soldiers with machine guns and tanks, next to text of Bible verses such as Ephesians, "Put on the full armor of God," and Psalms, "The eye of the Lord is on those who fear Him." Hypocritical? You be the judge.

Our finger-wagger is shooting multiplying fish in a barrel with a machine gun in their "pro-greed" allegation. The Bible comes down pretty clearly on this one: "It is easier for a camel to go through the eye of a needle, than for a rich man to enter into the kingdom of God." While said book is chock-full of even more dazzling miracles than nudging an animal through a needle's eye, the message is clear. It's just odd that so many Christians are so economically well off in light of the Bible's teaching, including the various mega-church evangelists earning upward of $3 million a year.

A more pressing question is: *Should* Christianity weigh in as it has on the death penalty, greed, war, etc.? This is a bit like asking George Lucas if *Star Wars* should send the message that it is sometimes permissible to kill your father, or even if the rim of a basketball hoop should stand ten feet from the floor. It's their game, and their rules. If one doesn't like the rules, one can invent a new game or play another. In the world of religion there are over a thousand games to play, including the actual Jedi Religion, which, according to the 2001 Census, has over 390,000 members in England, making it the country's fourth largest religion. They have yet to weigh in specifically on the death penalty, greed, and war, thus avoiding similar bumper-sticker attacks.

MY CHILD WAS . . . (HONOR STUDENT, BEST KID EVER, ETC.)

Okay, okay, we get it. Your child is better than mine. Not even that, it doesn't say "*I* Was the Best Ever," it says "*My* Kid Was," so it looks like you are (or at least were, according to the sticker's tense) a better parent than the rest of us. I'm okay with that. For those who are not okay, we have the strangely boastful,

MY CHILD BEAT UP YOUR HONOR STUDENT

and other like-minded versions, some even involving who's having sex with whom. Since "honor" in this case involves the giving of grades and assigning quality to students, let's look into the concept of *quality* driving all this to begin with.

These awards assume that we have a good grasp on "quality" and assigning value, though "quality" often varies in its application. A thing or activity can maintain an intrinsic value as something we value *in and of itself,* or a relative value as something we value *in relation to* other things of its kind. A billion dollars has great value for you now, but were you on a deserted island it wouldn't do you any more good than a pile of paper with which to make a fire one cold evening. So, it's valuable *relatively* speaking. Your grandfather's first handwritten poem, however, likely has very little worth on the open market but is potentially of great worth to your family, *intrinsically* speaking.

So who's assigning the quality and what do they mean by it? As Robert Pirsig writes of "quality" in his philosophical novel *Zen and the Art of Motorcycle Maintenance*, "You know what it is, yet you don't. If no one knows what it is, then for all practical purposes it doesn't exist at all. But for all practical purposes it really does exist. What else are the grades based on?" Maybe we should turn to the experts: college professors.

In 2000, researchers at Clarion University collected 120 term papers from students and had eight faculty members assign a grade to each paper. As you might imagine, the grades differed widely, averaging almost a full letter-score variance on a single essay, with some differing by two or more grades. So, if Professor X grades your papers, then you get A-'s and bumper stickers. If Professor Y, then C-'s. No bumper sticker for you, student of Professor Y—maybe you're the one beating up all of the honor students of X. Or having sex with them. Or at least printing up abrasive bumper stickers about them. It is understandably frustrating.

When it comes down to it, the school is the one printing the sticker and giving them out every week. So what's the kid supposed to do, just put it on his arithmetic binder with the rest of his smiley faces and gold stars?

MORALITY
Being Right About Moral Matters *Matters*

PRACTICE RANDOM ACTS OF KINDNESS AND SENSELESS ACTS OF BEAUTY

Along with randomly kind acts comes the onset of unselfish behavior, for no selfish person acts in such a manner. A warning: Some believe they have found a way to make the seemingly sel*fless* act non-existent. They do so by employing this semantic sleight of hand: All purposeful actions benefit the self by the mere fact of the self *wanting* to do them. On the TV sitcom *Friends,* Phoebe accuses Joey of acting in a morally impoverished, selfish manner for donating his time to PBS just to get on television. Joey then challenges her, claiming that no sel*fless* action is possible—for example, she carries the baby of her brother and his wife who are unable to have children but does so because she values helping a family member; she donates to charity and it makes her feel good. In the end, she is unable to find a truly selfless action. This cynicism likely causes the response to this bumper-sticker wisdom:

PRACTICE RANDOM AND SENSELESS ACTS

As is often the case, the antidote to poor reasoning is a good dose of logic. (Yum!) By using the word "selfish" to describe all possible actions, it renders the word useless. It's like using "natural" to describe artificial flavors on the basis of their composition including ingredients exclusively *from nature*. Where else would they come from? To have any meaning at all, a word must have at least the possibility of being used incorrectly.

In the iconoclastic Ayn Rand's aptly titled *The Virtue of Selfishness*, logic and reason drive her to defend selfishness—to help us avoid the typical ugliness we associate with it. One can achieve true happiness, she explains, only when the actor is "the beneficiary of his action," based on "his own *rational* self-interest." She suggests that blindly adhering to a duty of mindless altruism causes morality to be seen more as our enemy than as something we strive for. This results in people who do not value themselves intrinsically (and, incidentally, makes them incapable of love) and results in moral interactions more closely resembling "an exchange of unwanted, un-chosen Christmas presents." Instead of adhering to the bumper-sticker wisdom here, we need not make or accept sacrifices but only live for our own sake. Her view more closely resembles another bit of bumper-sticker wisdom:

PRACTICE PRINCIPLED ACTS OF SELF-INTEREST AND RUTHLESS LOGIC

Oh that Mother Teresa, so selfish, wanting to help other people all the time and journey to heaven for a while afterward. Yet her acts were hardly random or unplanned. Not very spur-of-the-moment. Maybe this bumper-sticker wisdom isn't for her. Her vow of poverty certainly prevented her from owning objects with bumpers for stickers anyway.

Now enter a more recent development in evolutionary theory—reciprocal altruism. "I'll scratch your back if you scratch mine," as they so eloquently pontificate in movies such as *Superbad*. Here's how it works: In your caveman clan, if you're a back-scratcher and your buddy Cromag is not, then when disaster strikes, who will have a better chance of surviving, acquiring food, caring for children, and eventually finding a mate? You will (and not just because you're so cute). So, over time, this favorable trait becomes passed on, and all of the selfish Cromags of the world die off before they can have and raise little Cromaggies, and *voilà*, we evolve a natural propensity for kindness. Even at the group level, clans of back-scratchers live on, while the ruthlessly selfish tribes die off. You're free to roll in the itchy grass as you see fit.

Scottish philosopher David Hume anticipated this as he wrote that acting morally is as much a part of nature as eating and mating: The emotion we feel upon doing good or contemplating an honorable character has been made universal in our species *by nature.* So it looks like this bumper sticker might as well say, "Practice Eating Three Square Meals a Day." While lack of food results in bodily death, a lack of kindness and morality results in existential, psychical death. This is the beauty of ethics: It teaches not so much how to stay alive, but how to truly live.

As for the randomness, it's hard to imagine what's so bad about practicing Organized, Ordered, Planned Acts of Kindness. And likewise the senselessness. So go ahead and plan the acts, and even have them make sense if you're so inclined.

RELIGION IS WHAT KEEPS THE POOR FROM MURDERING THE RICH

Recently parents have started installing surveillance cameras inside their teenagers' cars. The result: more buckled seat belts, less risky behavior, and fewer accidents. As a simple rule of human nature goes: If you believe you're being watched by an authoritative and caring being, you'll follow his or her rules. We would be seriously concerned about a driver who believed he was on film yet ran red lights, sped through residential streets, and drank alcohol while driving. The only real explanation being, he just must not believe he was being watched. This same line of reasoning applies to those who claim that an ever-present being constantly watches them yet choose to do other than what the being purportedly allows, especially when the punishment is infinitely worse than taking away one's car. The only viable explanation is that they don't really think He's there after all.

This bumper-sticker wisdom makes an assumption about morality and human nature, attempting to affirm the often misquoted words of Dostoyevsky, "Without God, everything is permissible." Yet for those who want ethics to be only God-given—the problem of deciphering which god notwithstanding—we must anticipate a resounding "Yes!" in response to the question "If it were proven to you that no God exists, would you start stealing, murdering, raping, and so on?" Yet no believer ever responds in such a manner. This, in itself, demonstrates that the "divine command theory" of morality isn't truly what motivates them. There must be something else driving morality.

Yet political leaders continue to apply this in a cause-and-effect analysis of crime. As then House Majority Leader Tom DeLay suggested, tragedies such as the 1999 Columbine massacre are perpetrated by an education system that teaches children that "They are nothing but glorified apes who evolutionized [sic] out of some primordial soup of mud." He takes the bumper-sticker non-wisdom one step further, as if to say: **"Teaching Children Myths Instead of Facts Is What Keeps the Poor from Murdering the Rich."**

A 2005 study in *The Journal of Religion and Society* surveyed over 800 million people from eighteen democratic countries to explore this very issue. They examined how "religiosity"—biblical literalism, belief in a creator, and frequency of prayer and religious service—correlates with "dysfunctionality," as demonstrated by homicide rates, suicide, life expectancy, STD infection, abortion, early pregnancy, and childhood mortality.

The United States scores highest in "religiosity," leading in the categories "Absolutely believe in God," "Take Bible literally," and "Pray at least several times a week" (though, oddly, not leading in "Attend religious services several times a month"). So our bumper-sticker owner must anticipate correlations that demonstrate greater moral purity. Yet (surprise, surprise) the United States also has the highest per-capita rates of homicide, childhood mortality, adolescent syphilis and gonorrhea infections, as well as abortions and teen pregnancies. As it turns out, the most secular, *pro*-evolution democracies exhibit the lowest rates of sexual dysfunction, lethal crime, and abortion. While Norway has an exceptionally high percentage of its population not believing in supernatural beings, the Global Peace Index rates them the most peaceful country in the world. The Human Development Index likewise has ranked them at the number one spot for the past five consecutive years. Fortunately, no leader in Norway has said what President George Bush-Take-One is reported as having said while on the campaign trail in 1987: "I don't know that atheists should be considered as citizens." These 40 million U.S. citizens can thank their lucky stars for the separation of church and state, though forfeiting citizenship would have at least saved them from having to pay taxes.

In recent history, secular humanism (sort of a code name for atheism) has appeared on the scene of moral discourse. The first Humanist Manifesto, written in 1933, served as a creed for humanists. It has since been updated and includes the charge to "lead ethical lives of personal fulfillment that aspire to the greater good of humanity," and commands a commitment to "treating each person as having inherent worth and dignity." The chair emeritus of the Council for Secular Humanism, Paul Kurtz, writes of humanism's core value as "the realization and enhancement of human fulfillment," which entails a need for "empathy, altruism, and good will." While the documents go into much greater detail, one can discern from even the brief excerpts here that these leading humanists hardly advocate the every-man-for-himself sort of moral vacuum which the religious suggest would occur without rulebooks from their respective Eye in the Sky.

Our bumper-sticker owner likely hoped to take a cheap shot at religion. In doing so he ironically frames one of the main defenses of religious groups. And it turns out that neither is right: Religion doesn't keep people from doing bad things nor are religious people any more moral than their counterparts. And thank goodness.

As Einstein quipped, "If people are good only because they fear punishment, and hope for reward, then we are a sorry lot indeed."

DON'T JUDGE ME

It's only a matter of time (hours, really) before someone touting this bumper-sticker command can be seen condemning a politician, choosing one person over another as a friend, voting, buying a song on iTunes, or just plain ol' complaining "This sucks"—all of which involve judging. This embodies that favorite rhetorical question typically posed by those acting immorally, "Who are *you* to tell me what's right and wrong?" It actually provides a great opportunity to illustrate an *ad hom* attack—short (and Latin) for, "At the man." That's just the point: "You" don't need to be anyone in particular to tell "me" what's right or wrong. That is, unless you're the leader of a cult or religion that has its own set of pseudo-moral rules to which we're not privy.

Imagine a conversation to the tune of this bumper-sticker wisdom:

> "Ya know, what Hitler did really was wrong, killing six million innocent people like that."
> "Tsk, tsk. Don't judge."

Judgment is exactly what we want from a set of morals and ethics. Don't we want someone to judge those who enslaved others or committed acts of terrorism in the name of religion—to have had a logical conversation about it, versus allowing this sort of cultural relativism to run rampant?

Paraphrasing St. Ambrose's bumper-sticker-style instructions to St. Augustine in A.D. 370 nicely summarizes cultural relativism, when he recommended, "When in Rome Do As the Romans Do." But the seriousness of cultural relativism runs much deeper than determining the days on which to avoid eating, as was the case with Augustine's comparing the different fasting rituals of Italy and Rome. Certain cultures permit serious rights violations such as female genital mutilation, slavery, violence toward women, cannibalism, and even infanticide (the properly derived academic word for "killing infants").

We can imagine the response to a cultural relativist through other bumper-sticker wisdom:

YOU CALL IT "IMPOSING MY MORALITY." I CALL IT "KNOWING RIGHT AND WRONG."

This bumper sticker assumes that a universal set of moral guidelines exists in which moral statements are true and false just like factual statements about the earth's shape—that even if you're of the biblical ilk that the earth is flat, it doesn't really matter what you think, it either is or it isn't (author's note: It isn't). Moral subjectivism and cultural relativism argue just the opposite—that morality more closely resembles comparing apples and oranges: You like apples and she likes oranges, your culture likes eating your dead (the Callatians) while theirs does not; yours often allows infants and the elderly to die in the snow (Eskimos) while theirs does not. It's all a matter of taste.

Twentieth-century Austrian philosopher Ludwig Wittgenstein takes down the moral subjectivist in one fell swoop. He first summarizes their position—"One would like to say: Whatever is going to seem right to me is right"—and then responds, "And that only means that here we can't talk about 'right.' " Having people haphazardly inventing moral rules to suit their needs is as ineffective as people playing a game while each making up their own individual rules—the game would cease to exist. And it turns out people don't really want this after all.

Heavy metal rockers Metallica perform what could be seen as

the moral subjectivist anthem, in which they repeatedly chant "So what?" following a list of immoral endeavors. A separate music video shows them celebrating a shoplifting spree ("So what," remember?). Yet in 1999, along comes Napster, which essentially allows fans to shoplift Metallica's music. The band leads the charge on a quest of moral righteousness demonstrating that "So what?" typically applies only when it's in the chanter's favor. Rock star counterparts Everclear scream out in concert to their crowd, "The only rules are: There are no rules!" Yet as concertgoers storm the stage, they instruct them, "Okay, you guys gotta back up now, everybody back up. Back up!" So much for "no rules." If only they'd applied a little bit of logic in the first place: "There are no rules" is itself a sort of rule, thus turning their intended theory of do-what-you-want moral subjectivism into nothing—nihilism—and then gives the rule maker no leg to stand on in the first place. It's reminiscent of why no one ever shows up for anarchy meetings.

In addressing the more alluring cultural relativism, philosopher James Rachels highlights problems that result if one truly accepts this notion that whatever a culture deems moral is moral:

> 1. We could never condemn another culture's actions—Their genocide would be just another matter of taste: "Hey, over here we just prefer our oranges to your apples."
> 2. We would have cultures vote to determine ethics—"Turns out, we've elected slavery and orange-eating as *right* for us, while equality and apples work for you."
> 3. There would be no sense of moral progress—Eliminating slavery in the United States wouldn't mean we are "better" now, just that we do things differently: "We prefer apples now unlike our orange-eating ways of yore."

Despite relativism's serious shortcomings, Rachels argues that we can learn something from it. First, we might share values across cultures more than we realize. The Callatians ate their dead in order to transmit wisdom across generations and as a sign of respect; nomadic Eskimos allowed for occasional infanticide as a last resort, because infanticide allows more to live than would otherwise, as their way of life "forces upon them choices that we do not have to make," Rachels says. Secondly, a deeper understanding of various cultures encourages us to become more empathetic and open-minded, though, of course, not absentminded; as he concludes, "We can accept these points without going on to accept the whole theory."

So judge away. And don't worry about "ye being judged" in the process. You actually want a society that does that. When Jesus qua philosopher warned potential judgers of the judging they would receive in return, he was speaking of avoiding hypocritical judging or menial judging along the lines of gossip, snap judgments, and catty banter. He himself judged quite a bit, condemning various ills of society and doing so in a way the Bible also instructs: "Don't judge unrighteously" and "Judge a righteous judgment."

With a rejection of moral relativism, we can continue the quest for universal moral truths. And still, some cultural awareness of manners and customs will behoove the considerate traveler. So when in Indonesia, hand objects to others with your left hand. And when in Thailand, don't wear shoes in someone's home. And when in Rome . . .

GOD AND RELIGION
The Supernatural, the Natural, and the *Extraordinarily* Natural

SUPERMAN IS MY COPILOT

In true "Everything I learned, I learned through superheroes" fashion, nineteenth-century German philosopher Friedrich Nietzsche dons a Superman costume and squares off against the Indiana Jones–clad Danish philosopher Søren Kierkegaard on the spiritual battlefield. We might imagine the philosophical conundrum, "If each were on your porch on Halloween night and you had but one Tootsie Roll left, to whom would you give it?"

Cashing in on some of the church's earlier errors—such as the failure to place the sun in the center of the solar system, denouncing evolution, and others—Nietzsche proclaimed his infamous statement "God is dead." En route to doing so, he called for a complete reevaluation of values, termed "transvaluation." Criticizing it as "a religion of pity," he despised Christianity's condemnation of sexual activity, the elevation of the meek over the strong, and what he perceived as a vengeful nature evidenced by the celebration of the prophesized violent Final Judgment Day. With a backward and oppressive value system that focused more on death and promises of a later life—what folksinger Woody Guthrie would call "pie in the sky"—Nietzsche viewed the institution as actually "hostile to life," describing Christianity as "the one immortal blemish of mankind."

So as not to come across as the consummate naysayer, Nietzsche provided an ideal for which to strive that he termed the Übermensch, or Superman. (*Über* has become part of the slang lexicon for "super" or "ultimate" as in, "That movie was übercool.") In lieu of seeking unknown future lives and otherworldliness, Nietzsche argued that we ought instead to focus on the *known* of this life on earth. We should not create fantasy worlds to abate our dissatisfactions but should instead address these deficiencies head-on. Because the Übermensch embraces his mortal life, the values that result will thus celebrate human existence per se, allowing mankind to thrive in pursuit of deeply enriching self-discovery. Nietzsche argued that one not only *could* attain this real-life superhero status, but should strive to do so. Somewhat ironically, the initial creation of the comic-book hero Superman resembled a *villain* much more in line with Nietzsche's Übermensch. In the end, Nietzsche's kryptonite turned out to be the very mortality that he celebrated, as can be seen in this "We'll see who gets the last word" genre of bumper-sticker wisdom:

"GOD IS DEAD."—NIETZSCHE
"NIETZSCHE IS DEAD."—GOD

Indiana Jones to the rescue. In the third film of the Indiana Jones tetralogy, our reason-driven professor finds himself on the edge of a precipice separating him from the Holy Grail. Unable to leap to the other side, he takes to heart his father's instructions, "You must believe, Indy," and steps out over the abyss to find that a bridge existed after all. In the absence of any clear evidence, he found truth—all he had to do was leap. The fact that the bridge was there anyway (and that this is a Hollywood film) notwithstanding, this leap of faith guided him to divinity.

For Kierkegaard, one doesn't acquire faith as a result of objective evidence. In his view, truth's subjective nature results in a *need* for faith. He wrote that any supposed certainty would not lead to "belief," in just the same way that one cannot really "believe" they hold a book while reading it—it is something they *know*. Instead, *because* one cannot truly know God, then one *must* believe. Thus he introduces his famous phrase "A leap to faith." (He never used "of," as he found it somewhat redundant.)

To fully embrace the paradoxical nature of religion—and in Kierkegaard's case, of Christianity—one must "leap" over the contradictions and illogic. As he explains, this is the only way to allow Jesus to exist as both a man and a God. It might also help one reconcile cartoon pseudo-hero Homer Simpson's concern that an all-powerful being could not create a burrito so hot that he couldn't eat it. But it clearly introduces a new problem, calling into question how much one should ignore the adage "Look before you leap." The religious leap of faith almost requires that one refrain from looking and just jump—a true "just do it" approach. We can imagine a reality television game show contest among "leapers" to see what breadth of a belief-chasm they can cross. The game show host could affix lie detectors to contestants as a sort of Slam Dunk Contest of Leaps of Faith. At some point, it seems as though we might want to condemn such blind leaps instead of assigning virtue to them.

It turns out that the statement "Kierkegaard is dead" is also true. So maybe our two trick-or-treaters could at least split the candy in half and we can stay tuned for the next episode.

RELIGIONS ARE JUST CULTS WITH MORE MEMBERS

In the profile section, Facebook provides an option for users to list "religious views" but none for "cult affiliation." Clearly social stigma is on the line with this distinction. And with tax-exemption up for grabs as well, we should examine this through the lens of the experts who study cults and religions from various social and academic perspectives—because if you ask a religious person to define "cult," you just might hear, "Everyone *else's* religion." It presents sort of a spiritual conflict of interest.

Cults, some suggest, conform less to the traditional beliefs of a community. So maybe religion is like the Major League of the Professional Belief System League—you can imagine the article heading: "Scientology Drafted from the Minors for Their PBSL Debut." And the Mormon Church giving advice to those in the Minors: "You should consider something like magic golden plates in New York that permit members to have multiple wives. Never mind that the guy who translated them to angels was convicted for being an imposter only four years earlier, and that no one has seen the plates because he gave them to the angels when he was done reading them. Your 'Coca-Cola is magic' thing won't get you to the Majors. And having your followers burn themselves to death was a bad idea too."

Most religions begin as cults, as Christianity was considered a cult in first-century Rome. It took a few centuries and a superstitious leader in Constantine for it to become the state religion. Cults just need to exhibit a little more of that virtuous patience.

Not happy with a spiritual-squatters'-rights criterion, cult expert Michael Langone suggests that cults "exploit members psychologically and/or financially," by way of "psychological manipulation" and creating "anxious dependency." Noted expert Louis West adds that cult members have an excessive "dedication to some person, idea or thing." He references popular methods of cult manipulation techniques such as information management, suspending critical judgment, and promoting total dependency on the group. Despite lawsuit threats from the church/cult of Scientology against any psychiatrist calling them a cult, West did just that at a major gathering of professionals, also calling Scientology's inventor, L. Ron Hubbard, "a quack and a fake," just in case he wasn't clear.

But these classifications don't seem to properly distinguish today's religions from cults. As for financial and psychological exploitation through psychological manipulation, to achieve the *good* afterlife ("celestial kingdom") as a Mormon and in many other Christian sects you must be baptized, and when baptized you must promise to give 10 percent of your money to the church. This is also

the case for earning acceptance into the temple endowment ceremony in which you need a "Recommend," yet to get this: Give 10
percent. Straight from Brigham Young we read that to make it to
the celestial kingdom and avoid the *bad* afterlife ("outer darkness"),
"It requires a strict obedience to every point of law and doctrine."
And from the doctrine we also read that a "standing law unto them
forever" demands "one tenth of all their interest annually."

For added psychological manipulation, religions don't need the
cultish aliens visiting on comets because they have the threat of
hellfire. If a religion has truly convinced you of eternal burning,
then you're looking out for your kids by scaring them half to death.
This maybe explains how we might see Andrea Yates through a
more, um, caring lens. Yates drowned her five children—Noah,
Paul, Luke, John, and Mary—to save them. As she calmly explained, her children "Stumbled because I was evil . . . They were
doomed to perish in the fires of hell." How did she know this? Her
pastor made clear that because of her lifestyle, they were all
"headed for hell"—but not if they died before they sin.

Popular science author and Oxford fellow Richard Dawkins
refers to any religious scare tactic as child abuse. He goes further
in arguing that it is as wrongheaded to call a child a "Mormon
baby" as it is to call him a "Republican baby," though even more so
as the former comes with the added threat of torture in hell forever. How could a one-year-old know if they believed in magic
plates or trickle-down economics? Dawkins shares numerous
cases of his attending churches in which adult members wear
frightening devil costumes in a "Hell House" designed to scare
children. One parishioner defended this, claiming, "If [the kids]
end up having nightmares as a result of experiencing this, I think
there's a higher good." A Hell House is not needed, though, as the
mere mention to a child of eternal torture seems to suffice. The joy
that many religious have in imagining others going to hell is odd,
to say the least. Exalted church leader St. Thomas Aquinas once ex-
uded, "That the saints may enjoy their beatitude and the grace of
God more abundantly, they are permitted to see the punishment of
the damned in hell." And in a more contemporary voice, that of

popular conservative pundit Ann Coulter: "I defy any of my co-religionists to tell me they do not laugh at the idea of Dawkins burning in hell." Thomas and Ann clearly view heaven as a sort of public torture viewing or sadistic comedy club. Maybe we missed the punch line.

In a final attempt to sort out this bumper-sticker wisdom, sociologist Benjamin Zablocki suggests that one characteristic of cults involves their willingness to abuse members, especially sexually, through the spiritual power-position of the leader. For how could one—especially a child—say "no" to the man (always a man) holding the key to the afterlife? The wife of Raëlism's founder shared that her husband, Raël, had sex with hundreds of his young cult members. A proverbial Sherlock Holmes, she shared, "I began to think the whole Raëlian movement was a trick to have more sex." A trick, yes, or more of a ruse. Branch Davidian leader David Koresh married girls as young as twelve. The Old Testament draws the line here—you have to draw the line somewhere. No tax-exempt status there. Though without getting into too much detail, given the recently confirmed sexcapades of nearly five thousand priests with thousands of young children, this at least matches the practice of hundreds coerced into sexual relationships by cult leaders.

So maybe it is true: Cults just need to be patient and wait it out before they join rank with the hundreds of current religions. Or, as some suggest, the only criterion for entry in the Majors is simply to posit a supernatural being. So hurry up and invent one. A Flying Spaghetti Monster? "Approved." Welcome to the Majors.

BEER IS PROOF THAT GOD LOVES US AND WANTS US TO BE HAPPY

This bumper-sticker wisdom nearly unanimously comes in quotes and with the attribution "—Benjamin Franklin" under it, though wrongly so. Though Ben did make the same proclamation about wine in a letter to a cohort in which he hoped to defend the claim "Truth is in wine," and in which he expounded upon the miracle of turning water into wine as the roots of the grapevine absorb rainwater. In line with this bumper-sticker wisdom, the first beer, *ale,* was initially aligned with sorcery and magic and even thought to instill supernatural powers in the drinker. Then along came the wet blanket of science, illuminating the natural causes of that magical feeling which results from imbibing. Having now shed light on this attempt to demonstrate God's existence and His desires for us, not surprisingly many others have done considerably more work. In an Olympics of Proving God's Existence sort of way, the medalists of such an event might provide more insight on the topic.

One can't have such a discussion without mentioning eighteenth-century apologist William Paley's infamous watch analogy. In his book *Natural Theology,* he provides a "teleological argument": Derived from the Greek *telos,* this argument relies on a thing's having a *goal* or *purpose* and thus a creator who intended that. Paley discusses a watch and reminds us of its fine-tuned nature, clear purpose, and unique complexity. Clearly, the odds of something with such features coming into existence by mere chance would be so excruciatingly low that we must rule it out. The sure cause of such an item must then be a creator—a watchmaker—and an intelligent one no less. Applying this analogy to the universe, it has been argued that it too has a finely tuned nature, exquisite complexity, and, of course, a purpose: to have us in it. Thus, it too must have been designed.

On the pedestal with Paley, St. Thomas Aquinas offered numerous proofs of God's existence. Both his first and second attempts are quite similar, involving the concepts of motion and causation. He holds that no thing can cause itself: For a thing to do that would require that the object in question achieve the logical impossibility of existing before itself. He then argues that the backward tracing of causes—i.e., your parents caused you, their parents caused them, etc.—cannot continue infinitely because then there would be no first cause to eventually cause our existence. And thus, to put it bluntly, "It is necessary to admit a first . . . cause, to which everyone gives the name God." In the thir-teenth century, this truly was the name to which nearly everyone gave such a concept.

And thirdly, in no specific order—you can determine for your-self the respective placement of our God Proving medalists—hail-ing from the twelfth century, philosopher and theologian Anselm of Canterbury (so as not to be confused with all the other Anselms). Anselm popularized the "ontological argument" for God's exis-tence—ontology being the study of existence. In what feels like a logical sleight of hand, Anselm cleverly delivers his proof of God's existence in a "right before your very eyes" sort of way. He first has us agree that God is a being about which nothing greater can be imagined. Even if you don't currently believe God exists, you know what we're talking about, and you know that He is perfect, by defi-nition. And since existing trumps not-existing, God must exist. What good would a perfect being be if it didn't exist? In lacking any favorable quality, that particular being wouldn't be perfect and, thus, wouldn't be God to begin with. Therefore, this perfect being, God, not only exists but does so necessarily.

In light of our bumper-sticker wisdom, these arguments at-tempt "merely" to prove God's existence and not to demonstrate how He feels about us. Though clearly, before someone loves us they must first exist—this simple bit of logic won't be lost on any-one. And as the astute reader likely anticipates, many philoso-phers, scientists, and even theologians have expressed concerns with these arguments, and have also offered various arguments to the contrary. But also in light of this sticker, if having a beer or a glass of wine makes you happy, cheers.

INTELLIGENT DESIGN IS NEITHER

Clever: separately negating both of the words in a phrase. Maybe it's meant metaphorically. That same negation-game would work with "Dead Ringer" and "Lame Duck." If meant as a mere metaphor, then we should examine what possible kernel of truth hides within—looking first to see if something/someone designed everything and, if so, what that designer would be like.

In a letter to a friend, Charles Darwin wrote, "What a book a Devil's Chaplain might write on the clumsy, wasteful, blundering low and horridly cruel works of nature." Assuming that a supernatural being willingly designed things, we can learn much about this supposed being's qualities—that is, if He is actually loving, smart, powerful, and so on. If this being turns out to be "clumsy, wasteful . . . and horridly cruel," then we must either reject said being altogether or at least restructure the adjectives typically used to describe the design.

That said, imagine how an "Intelligent Designer" might have thought through some of these so-called designs in light of Darwin's description:

Horridly Cruel: "I'll design a parasite that needs to get into the stomach of a cow or sheep to live. To get there, I'll have it burrow into the brain of an ant—note to self, design ants—forcing the ant to climb atop grass to be more easily killed and eaten by the cows. And then I'll design most of the animals so that they eat their victims alive. Even chimpanzees can pin down smaller, screaming monkeys while they tear flesh from their body. And I'll design the female praying mantis so that she eats the male immediately after coitus and sometimes just before so as to create a residual thrashing motion. Female black widows can bite the head off their partners after a roll in the sack. Maybe this will make cuddling seem more appealing to the human animals I'll make in a few days."

Wasteful: "I'll design things so that 99 percent of species that ever live will go extinct." (Need we say more on the wastefulness? It makes consumer America look like one big Green Party.)

But just because someone creates things that lead to great waste and cruelty, that doesn't necessitate that He's not intelligent. After all, it's not called the "Cruel Design Theory." So, how about that criterion of "Intelligent"?

Intelligent: The movie *Dogma* opens with the text "Even God has a sense of humor. Just look at the platypus." But a designer of good humor is a highly evolved horse of another color compared to being intelligent—it's not "Humorous Design Theory" either. But only the best science-fiction writer could explain the intelligence of putting leg bones on whales: In case the oceans dry up, they can acquire lungs and walk around. And maybe giving ostriches and emus wings—even if they can't fly—at least allows them to fit in with the other birds, though imagine the angst they must feel along with the aptly named blind mole rat that does have eyes that are covered with skin. As for wisdom teeth, it's hard to imagine the wisdom in that one, unless as a means for helping the profession of dentistry.

One can't look into "intelligent" design without glancing at male mammal nipples. It's difficult to do research on these as mammals leave behind no nipple fossils. Male mammals have useless nipples—except that silly platypus in which neither male nor female bothers—and possums can have up to twenty-five of them. Another creator decided they weren't important: Neither Barbie nor Ken has nipples. So the bumper-sticker non-wisdom strangely flaunted by some women that they either hate Barbie or want to be her because she apparently has "*everything*" turns out not to be true either. But it's literally no skin off men's backs having them, so why not? We still have toenails yet we don't dig and scratch with them like other mammals.

Lastly, we reflect on the eyeball. The vertebrate eye is designed about as backward as possible, with the light traveling through various parts of the eye to get to the light-receiving cells. The supposed design includes a blind spot in our visual field and also various common complications causing visual impairment. If a university were to hold an engineering contest to design the most efficient, "intelligent" mechanism for vision, the human eye would finish near last place. Though, interestingly, the "designer" of the squid eye produced just the opposite, more efficient version—maybe the Designer is a squid.

Certainly a creator *could* have designed all of this, but a bottom-up style of creation like evolution would *only* have done this. Some creationists reference the banana as proof: It fits perfectly into our hand, has a tab for easy opening, and is perfect for eating. Yet they fail to mention the pineapple, artichoke, and various other culinary challenges, and they also overlook the irony that the banana actually evolved from the less palatable plantain. So maybe the Intelligent Designer had a sense of humor after all, and He allowed the banana to evolve for all of the Three Stooges–style slippery-banana-peel jokes. The "design" portion of the bumper sticker is literally a question of faith—because if you leave it up to the facts, the scientists, and the courts of law, they rule heavily against it. Intelligent, cruel, and wasteful? Maybe just a matter of taste, though we do have more data than if we were just comparing evolutionarily engineered apples to oranges.

WHEN YOU PRAY GET OFF YOUR KNEES

No, this wasn't extracted from a "How to Pray Effectively" pamphlet displaying effective prayer positions. It's more along the lines of that ol' motivational saying "The harder I work, the luckier I get." No luck, just hard work. And the other bumper-sticker wisdom, "Peel off that yellow ribbon and *do* something!"—as if paying a dollar for this ribbon absolves one from doing anything else. Here is where the Lance Armstrong story intersects these three concepts: Establish a yellow-wrist-band-selling foundation for curing cancer that you yourself defeated, get off your knees, work hard, and win an unprecedented seven consecutive Tours de France. And what does he have to say about it? "If there was a God, I'd still have both nuts." Just imagine what he could have accomplished with the added supernatural power of prayer. As former slave Frederick Douglass said, "I prayed for freedom for twenty years, but received no answer until I prayed with my legs." (Again, not another prayer position.)

But because "to pray" derives from "to ask or request," this bumper sticker essentially requests that you stop requesting. Admittedly, it initially seems like a strange cause to promote. What could really be the harm? The harm is in thinking that praying actually does something, as highlighted by numerous recent examples of parents merely praying for their children suffering from curable diseases, rather than seeking medical care, thus resulting in their death. Comedian-turned-evangelical-atheist Julia Sweeney shares her concern regarding people who pray for starving children in Africa and, ten minutes later—after forty-two have died of starvation—they believe they've actually done something for them, and they carry on with their day. It's like a parent asking their child if he cleaned his room and he responds, "No, but I thought about it," only a lot more serious.

But prayer must "work," right? Not according to a recent study, conducted by both religious and non-religious doctors at Harvard University and published in the *American Heart Journal*. Researchers examined participants who were undergoing a specific type of heart surgery, dividing them into three groups: control (the regular group, hanging out in the hospital), the secretly prayed-for (three congregations prayed for these patients but they didn't tell the patient), and the more explicit, "You're being prayed-for" group. Not only was there no healing power afforded to either prayed-for group, but the knowingly prayed-for patients suffered *more* complications. One researcher surmises, "It might have made them uncertain, wondering, 'Am I so sick they had to call in their prayer team?' " Either that, or the people praying in that group just aren't that good at prayer. For now, it looks like doctors won't be prescribing prayer anytime in the near future. The new malpractice suit: "That doctor said he had people praying for me."

But the Bible clearly states, "You will receive whatever you ask for in prayer," and "Nothing will be impossible to you." But what of the thousands who die every day of hunger despite the millions of prayers to "End World Hunger"? And, as other poignant bumper-sticker wisdom asks,

WHY WON'T GOD HEAL AMPUTEES?

Feeding hungry people hardly seems impossible, and re-growing a limb not nearly as difficult as making dead people alive. The problem here is that things that would have happened regardless of prayer are often attributed to prayer. Sometimes cancer naturally goes into remission, yet we hear about the one who prayed for it and not the others. Sometimes both the batter and pitcher pray, yet we only hear from the batter whose prayers were answered with a home run—or from the pitcher if the batter strikes out. Thus far, not a single amputee has had that prayer answered.

Late 1800s American writer Ambrose Bierce once wrote that to pray is "to ask that the laws of the universe be annulled on behalf of a single petitioner confessedly unworthy." But it doesn't have to be. It can also be something more along the lines of "a nice quiet moment to reflect on all of one's good fortune, give thanks, and mentally dictate a sort of journal-entry in one's head." Meditation, yoga, and quiet walks on the beach have all been shown to have positive physiological effects—though it might seem strange if your friend well-wishes you by saying, "I yoga-ed for you today," or "I would love to help your father. I will go meditate for him." Recall the old adage "Two hands working can do more than a thousand clasped in prayer"—so imagine what a thousand and two hands could do.

FUNDAMENTALISM STOPS A THINKING MIND

Philosopher Bertrand Russell once wrote, "Many people would sooner die than think. In fact, they do." Fundamentalism epitomizes a virus of the mind, causing this very I'd-rather-die-than-think sort of problem. In short, fundamentalism is total adherence to a religious/cult-style set of beliefs, taking what the texts and religious leaders say as literally true without any reflection or skepticism (or thinking). Often used synonymously with dogmatism, the fundamentalist holds *dogma*—non-provable theoretical statements—as truth. It's a sort of spiritual totalitarianism that relies on various concepts like eternal damnation, unquestionable dogma, an ever-present "eye in the sky," oppression of women, and a little guilt.

Then again, thinking requires a lot of work. For the fundamentalist to weigh in on ethical issues, there is no need for thinking. When asked about their stance on cloning, they simply respond, "I'm not sure, I have to check such and such a book and then I'll tell you." And "How should we treat our homosexual neighbors?" elicits the response, "Let me see what my leader or book says to do." When Pope Alexander VII asserted that the idea of the earth orbiting the sun "is false and altogether incompatible with divine Scripture," or when he receives any other scientifically contradictory interpretations, a fundamentalist must side with his religion. And clearly the attacks on September 11 and others like them as per religious fundamentalism cannot embody what we value in the adjective "thinking." For the fundamentalist, there's no questioning the Koran's command to "make war on the unbelievers and the hypocrites and deal rigorously with them." Thus, the meat behind author Sam Harris's controversial pronouncement of the September 11 terrorists as neither cowards nor lunatics but, unfortunately for us, men of "perfect faith."

Fundamentalists encounter a real challenge when they attempt to disagree with their holy book or the divinely inspired leader. For Catholics to dispute the pope's stance on gay marriage, for example, they would have to think that this person who communes with God is actually wrong. Here fundamentalists face a serious dilemma: Hold tightly to the literal word of the text and of God, which often leads to atrocities (but makes one a good fundamentalist), or interpret it as you wish, thus admitting that either God was wrong, or the writers got it wrong, or God can sometimes be ignored.

In a less harmful example, the Catholic Church demands adherents' belief in the literal changing of bread to flesh, and wine to blood: what they aptly call "transubstantiation." The result of the consecration ceremony is not merely a symbol of Christ, as in the Protestant Church, but *is* this man, containing no bread whatsoever, as per the Catholic Church's Council of Trent decree. The catechism cites St. Cyril, who instructs us, "Do not doubt whether this is true." If you, the reader, don't believe in this, then you know where they think you'll be spending your afterlife. The real interest here lies in the forcing of one to believe in something as fantastic as this. Successful substance-changing of this sort goes against all immutable laws of the universe and would make Houdini and David Copperfield look like amateur magicians. As Harris again wryly notes in *The End of Faith,*

> Tell a devout Christian that his wife is cheating on him . . .
> and he is likely to require as much evidence as anyone
> else. . . . Tell him that the book he keeps by his bed was
> written by an invisible deity who will punish him with fire
> for eternity if he fails to accept its every incredible claim
> about the universe, and he seems to require no evidence
> what so ever.

Unfortunately, fundamentalism causes harm not only to oneself but to others, as is certainly evident in recent holy wars and terrorist activity, though it permeates more than just large-scale events. Even currently, children repeatedly die easily preventable deaths because parents opt to simply pray in lieu of pursuing simple medical treatment. Somehow legislatures continue to support this situation under the umbrella of "religious freedom" (despite its not seeming very "freeing" for the child), as we hear from a former Florida mayor and End Times fundamentalist: "It may be necessary for some babies to die to maintain our religious freedoms."

It is said that all sins can be forgiven, though this clearly does not seem accurate. As for one who has ever doubted God or called into question His existence, we read in Mark 3:29 that "whoever blasphemes against the Holy Spirit will never be forgiven, but is guilty of an eternal sin." That seems straightforward: Any sorts of blasphemous thoughts render it *impossible* for the one having the thoughts—the "thinker"— to earn forgiveness and thus avoid hell. With that in place, it's hard to imagine that anyone over five years of age ever gets to heaven. (If it makes any difference, I forgive you.)

JESUS SAVES . . . HE PASSES TO GRETZKY . . . GRETZKY SHOOTS . . . HE SCORES!

It's hard to tell just whose side this sticker owner is really on. Most of the "Jesus Saves" sport-related stickers have him passing to Moses or Noah, so it's like this true *fan*atic of ice hockey and religion put the two *greats* on one team. Though this wouldn't fit on a sticker: "Jesus saves, passes to Moses, who skates around for forty days and forty nights, then, parting the ice with his stick, walks it into the goal." But with all of the important things going on in the universe, it just seems that the gods wouldn't care much about guys skating around hitting vulcanized rubber into nets (or, in Jesus' case, keeping it out) or hitting balls over fences with sticks, and so on.

When you look at the actual sporting world, you find something different. Take the 2007 Super Bowl. *God,* the *Lord,* and the less conventional *Football Gods* received numerous shout-outs from players, coaches, commissioners, and commentators on this earthly day of rest. This should come as a surprise given that the winning team had sixty actual human players (including the "most valuable" player) who devoted their lives to getting the pigskin into the end zone. We must also assume that none of the gods involved took issue with these players handling swine. It is curious that God would look so favorably on all of these creatures doing anything but resting on the Sabbath.

Interestingly, there was very little mention of God from the los-ing side. This is consistent with the God of Sports who typically re-ceives accolades for successes (e.g., Bonds's point-to-the-sky instead of pointing to his steroid-pushing trainer, or genuflections and signs of the cross following a touchdown or home run) but no gratitude at times of failure (e.g., the oft-utilized "Damn it!" follow-ing a dropped ball or strikeout).

But since the God of most religions is omnipresent, it is not much of an issue that He was present at the Super Bowl. High school sports must observe strict secular rules to adhere to the day of rest, so this really would allow the gods to focus on this particu-lar event. Most of the gods currently posited *could* work at football games while still aiding the impoverished in Tanzania and answer-ing the prayers of roulette players in Las Vegas.

This all assumes that God plays an active role not only in the universe but on the sports field, and that God really can help a re-ceiver catch an otherwise un-catchable ball, or a defensive back to tackle an un-prayed-for running back. Given this assumption— that God overturns the supposedly immutable laws of nature— what we really witness at the Super Bowl are numerous small miracles: events that occur solely due to divine intervention.

While a recent religious-funded Harvard University study showed prayer to be ineffective in regard to healing the sick, it could be that God plays a more active role in the sporting realm, though it's hard to imagine that His priorities are as out of wack as ours here on earth. A similar study would be interesting: asking congregations to pray for one team's victory (and subsequently, an-other team's loss) while still accounting for the numerous con-founding variables such as home-court advantage, "the sun was in our eyes," and of course, *skill*.

Were the gods involved in sport, we'd expect religious universi-ties to prevail, yet that is far from the case. The Director's Cup is awarded annually to the university with the top overall athletic pro-gram, accounting for all sports played at each university, male and female, including every college in the United States. In the fifteen years of its existence, no religious-based university has finished even in the top five. In 2008 the highest-ranking religious-affiliated school was Notre Dame's Fighting Irish, draped in official school colors of "Madonna Blue" and "Papal Gold," coming in at twenty-first. And while we can imagine the cry from the religious—"But *they* have better athletes, more money, lower academic standards"—that shouldn't hold a candle in Candlestick Park to the athletic prowess of an *all-powerful* team member.

Regardless of who saves, scores, strikes out, or body-slams, it looks like we might need to go back to something a little more tangible in our trying to figure out why the ball or puck ended up where it did: human intervention.

"THE FISH BOWL"—
⊂×, ETC.

The Ichthys Fish derives from a mathematical co-joining of two circles which serves as an important symbol in many ancient religions. The fishiness derives from Ichthys, the son of the sea goddess Aphrodite.

In the first century, the Ichthys Fish served as both an identifier for Christians hoping to secretly distinguish themselves as true believers, and in place of an arrow (the head being the "pointer") to guide other believers to secret meetings, hoping to avoid persecution. Since Americans no longer persecute believers, nor burn heretics for that matter, people can freely share their religion on, what else, the backs of cars. Recently, these symbols have developed into somewhat of an ongoing conversation about cosmology—how things came to be. In examining the meaning of many of these, we can take a brief tour through the landscape of ideas on this topic:

Fish symbol: God—the Christian god—created everything just as it is in its current form.

 Fish with "Thor" in it: God—the Germanic god, Thor—created everything just as it is in its current form.

 Fish smoking a pipe with "Rasta" in it: God—the Christian god of Rastafarianism—created everything just as it is in its current form, "And it was ire."

 Fish made into a Spaghetti Monster creature with "FSM" in it: God—the Flying Spaghetti Monster—created everything with his "Noodly Appendage."

 Fish made into a Unicorn: God—the Invisible Pink Unicorn—created everything just as it is in its current form.

 Fish with "Truth" in it: God—the Christian god—created everything just as it is in its current form. This is True, so you can't argue with it.

 Six fishes with "Yahweh," "God," "Gaia," "Allah," "Tao," and "Other" in them all in a circle with "Go Fish" in the middle: It's about as easy to prove one god's existence over another so, "Go Fish."

In the interest of space, one can simply place any of the thousand or so possible gods' names inside the fish, thus announcing who/what one thinks created everything.

 Fish with legs: The Christian god created everything by using evolution.

 Fish with "Darwin" in it: Darwin's highly confirmed process of Natural Selection resulted in life.

Fish with "N' Chips" in it: Clever way of saying the English delicacy "Fish n' Chips."

 Fish with "Gefilte" in it: Clever way of saying the Jewish delicacy "Gefilte Fish."

 Fish symbol with "Ixoye" in the middle: God created everything just as it is in its current form. With "Ixoye" being an acronym in Greek for "Jesus Christ, God's Son, Savior," he too was involved. (*Ixoye* also means "fish," which is apt, albeit a bit redundant, its being *in* a fish.)

 Fish with "Ixoye" in it being eaten by a fish with "Science" in it: God created everything just as it is in its current form; no, wait, now we have evidence that everything evolved. Plus, many people eating fish.

 Fish holding a wrench with "Evolve" in it: Humans evolved to the point where we can now tighten bolts on our cars, kudos to the opposable thumb.

 Dinosaur eating the fish: Dinosaurs actually did roam the earth as the fossils show, and the "fish symbol theory" is tasty but not true.

 Fish with "Truth" in it eating a Darwin fish: I said, the Christian god created everything just as it is in its current form. End of story. Do you really want to disagree with me?

 Evolution fish having intercourse with the Ixoye fish: Regardless of one's beliefs, we are all here today because of sex. Also, interfaith marriage is now permitted.

GOD SAID IT. I BELIEVE IT. THAT SETTLES IT.

Loud and clear. (Note to any first-year high school teachers looking for an example to teach "dogmatism," look no further.)

Just a few quick questions regarding these three statements.

Which God? Hopefully not the one in the Bible who wants to have us stoned to death for gathering sticks on the weekend. Nor the Christian sect of Rastafarianism that commands us to smoke marijuana in order to talk to him (though ten thousand people at a recent concert may argue differently). Nor the New Testament one who prohibits our two nice neighbors from marrying each other because they unconditionally love the wrong people. Nor the one of Scientology that claims we have to give a bunch of money to the OT III–level church members so they can remove the spirits of space aliens that have inhabited our bodies, causing psychological angst.

And who are "you" and what other things do you believe? That is, what makes someone an expert on certain gods or other stories? Richard Dawkins wryly comments, "It assumes that there is a serious subject called Theology," and then asks, "Would you need to read learned volumes on Leprechology before disbelieving in leprechauns?" Then again, in 2005 the community council of St. Fillans, Perthshire, ordered the ceasing of a construction project in which $30,000 worth of time and goods had been invested because they believed it would disrupt fairies living under nearby rocks. This all transpired without consulting a single Fairyologist.

Lastly, what exactly is "it" that has been *settled,* anyway? What is *it*?

In an interesting turn of events comes the following bumper-sticker wisdom in response:

MY KARMA RAN OVER YOUR DOGMA

Karma typically doesn't play the role of spiritual bulldozer. Often allied with a non-violent way of life, this bumper-sticker wisdom actually seems to employ the wrong verb—maybe "Quieted" or "Pacified" works better than "Ran Over." A primary Buddhist and Hindu tenet, the karma or "action" of the universe accounts for the overarching "oneness" deeply entrenched in their view of reality— one's actions in this life determine the fate of one's soul in the next. Yogi Sri Tulsidas informs us, "Our destiny was shaped long before the body came into being." Those in the Western world often joke about another's acting immorally, "Oh, you're going to come back as a cockroach in your next life." This sort of karmic retribution— something along the lines of *Radiohead*'s "Karma Police"—serves as a moral motivator for action. No one wants to spend a few weeks as a cockroach, so be kind to others and don't tell lies.

But this introduces an odd twist when taken seriously and applied to those in a current state of crisis. Imagine the young child nearly starving to death with no family member to comfort him. Through this karmic lens, we must assume that the soul of this individual did something horrendous in a past life and now serves the assigned penalty in this state of affairs—deserves it, even. Sort of a penalty box for the soul, as though they "got what's coming to them." Maybe this is what the courts mean when they assign someone a 200-year prison sentence: that it applies to their next life as well, inside the "prison" of some less fortunate being. So in the case that "My Car Ran Over Your Dog"—the only potentially punny value of this sticker—then the dog must have done more than the moral equivalent of just chewing shoes in his past life. Bad dog.

English writer Douglas Jerrold once suggested, "Dogmatism is puppyism come to its full growth." That's just silly. But from one in the running for the title "Father of Modern Medicine," William Osler instead advised, "The greater the ignorance the greater the dogmatism." That seems a little closer to a true insight.

THEY CALL IT CREATION SCIENCE BECAUSE IT'S ALL MADE UP!

No, "they" call it that as the proverbial wolf in sheep's clothing trying to pull the wool over our eyes. They actually call it Creation *Science* for a very simple reason—if it is "science" then it must be taught in *science class*. Thus Zeus is never taught in science class; it's not "Zeus Science." If it were, then we would teach it in science class alongside other theories of thunder and lightning. But it's not, so we can't. We're not all sheep.

With nearly half of the U.S. population still believing that everything was created a few thousand years ago, and pretty much as it is now—ignoring the facts of evolution—wouldn't it be nice if we could put creationism on trial and finally get to the bottom of the controversy? Fortunately, this has happened on numerous occasions. This sort of trial actually happens on a daily basis in science labs everywhere, and has since the publication of Darwin's *The Origin of Species*. This is what scientists do: They put theories on trial. And they nearly unanimously agree that the theory of evolution has been substantially confirmed.

Additionally, creationism has literally been on trial repeatedly. In 1987, the Supreme Court ruled 7–2 against creationism being taught, as it clearly violates the First Amendment's Establishment Clause that prohibits forcing kids to adhere to the religious beliefs of their science teacher. Creationists were barred from using their book *Of Pandas and People* to teach human origins because it relied on religious "creationism." So they pulled the ol' switcharoo and published a second edition of the book, using the words "Intelligent Design" in place of "Creationism." "See, now it's not a religious *creator* but instead, some sort of intelligent design. We're teaching 'Intelligent Design *Science*.' " This is strangely similar to the Monty Python skit in which a fish owner crosses out the word "Cat" on his "Cat License" and writes the word "Fish" above it, thus creating (in his mind, at least) a Fish License.

So with the new crossed-out version of the so-called science book, a Pennsylvania Supreme Court re-examined creationism eighteen years later. After hearing extensive testimony on both sides from scientists, philosophers, and creationists, the Bush-appointed judge seemed to think the whole trial more resembled a Monty Python episode. He clearly ruled that not only is creationism not science but that evolution is "overwhelmingly accepted by the scientific community." He referred to the school board in Dover that attempted the ruse as "ill-informed" for adopting an "imprudent and ultimately unconstitutional policy." He noted that the decision for them to adopt this creationist book was one of "breathtaking inanity" resulting in an "utter waste of monetary and personal resources." To add to it all, it turned out that church donations paid for the public school's new-and-not-so-improved books. This especially angered the otherwise jovial judge, as this information was explicitly left out of the earlier testimony. Does "Thou shalt not bear false witness" include little white false witness? Guilty as charged.

With a majority of Americans unaware of DNA being the foundation of heredity, it's no surprise they don't agree with evolution, as they often don't know what it is. Anti-evolution creationists can be heard giving critiques that epitomize a straw man argument: "If evolution is true, why don't we see half-human/half-apes?" Answer: Because things evolve through generations, not within a single lifetime. So this majority wants the two taught together. Talk about the inmates running the asylum. President Bush even demanded this and was hardly challenged by voters when he did so. Imagine a bureaucrat overriding scientific facts about the universe, mandating what should be taught instead. Were it any of the other creation myths, equally unsupported, the outcry would be substantial: "President Tom Cruise should not be allowed to brainwash our children with his religious myths of Scientology. Separation of Church and State!" But when President Bush muses something along the lines of, "Aww, those science folks. Always saying that we came from apes and that we can't find a soul-thing in stem cells that are just like tiny people," we accept it.

"Teaching the controversy" shouldn't fly in a science class—or, it should "fly" like an early attempt at an airplane before the Wright Brothers used science to get it airborne. First of all, no controversy exists. And imagine telling children, "Here, kids: Seven guesses as to how humans came into existence. You choose. And that concludes your 'education' on the topic. Next we'll talk about all of the fun guesses as to why things fall toward the earth when released." Then we really could spend less on education and just have them watch Monty Python videos. And while they're at it, maybe they can solve that age-old question "How many angels can dance on the head of a pin?" For now, learning our actual origins through the non-made-up science might do us all a bit of good. As Will Smith reminisces in the opening of a music video of his, "My daddy told me one time, you don't know where you're going until you know where you've been."

GOD, PLEASE SAVE ME FROM YOUR FOLLOWERS!

A favorite strategy of atheist writers involves listing the abundantly horrendous evils committed by the religious in the name of religion. As the esteemed Steven Pinker writes, "Religions have given us stonings, witch-burnings, crusades, inquisitions, jihads, fatwas, suicide bombers, and abortion clinic gunmen." Religious writers employ a similar tactic in which, for example, the equally esteemed Dinesh D'Souza explains the likes of the non-religious (yet also Communist) Stalin, Mao Zedong, and Pol Pot, among others, including a running total of the millions killed by each.

Getting an accurate death toll from the two camps proves to be surprisingly difficult. More esteemed authors estimate that the Inquisition of the Catholic Church yielded 300,000 killed for the crime of "heresy," otherwise known as "not doing what the Church tells you to." This witch-hunt of sorts (not to be confused with the literal "Witch Trials") spanned nearly seven hundred years under the leadership of seventy popes, including the likes of Pope Innocent IV, who decreed that anyone who has allegedly gone against the church must be tortured until they admit to it, upon which the church will then hold a mass and kill them. At the least, it seems he could have chosen a name other than "Innocent." Yet, as D'Souza notes, historians argue that no more than 4,000 were killed by the church in the Inquisitions. Just 4,000 killed in the name of religion, not 300,000. That's a lot of esteem for such a major discrepancy. And when you add all of the religious-based violence from the Aztecs through today's ongoing feuds to the Crusades and on through present-day jihads and fatwas, the numbers reach into the millions. But all of this is rather moot to begin with as it boils down to an argument of principle in which the numbers are not as relevant as the motivation behind them.

D'Souza often asks his audiences, in his playful yet rigorous style, why so many people have published books arguing against God, citing the more popular *The God Delusion* and *God Is Not Great*. "Why not books arguing against the existence of unicorns?" he asks, rhetorically—though don't expect *The Unicorn Delusion* and *Unicorns Are Not Great* to hit bookstores soon. But unicorns have never driven people to kill on their behalf, nor to instigate wars among countries, nor to take rights from others, nor to condemn them to eternal torture. The "mere" 4,000 purportedly killed in the Inquisition already trump the number of unicorn-inspired deaths.

The concern from the religious is that atheism or its milder form, naturalism (that all things have natural causes, that we result from natural selection, etc.), also causes people to do bad things. The religious often reference all of the atheists on death row as proof, yet fail to note that a huge majority of felons have been religious. The clear difference, though, is that a non-believer doesn't commit crimes *on behalf of* not believing in something. Nearly all death-row inmates also don't believe in Zeus, Buddha, fairies, unicorns, or thousands of other things. At least 99 percent of murderers are aZeusists—they do not believe in Zeus—yet no one suggests that this non-belief somehow *causes* their wrong-doing. One just doesn't kill in the name of nothing or unbelief, as people have in the name of a particular god.

To update the scorecard tally: The Numbers Killed in the Name of:

> Religion: 1 million give or take.
> Nothing: 0.

But the anti-evolution religious faction often parades the words of horrendous serial killer Jeffrey Dahmer: "If a person doesn't think there is a God to be accountable to, then what's the point of trying to modify your behavior . . . ? I always believed the theory of evolution as truth." And then more from pseudo-comedian turned pseudo-scientist Ben Stein: "Science leads you to killing people." If this is true, then schools need to seriously reevaluate their science curriculum.

But over two hundred years ago Scottish philosopher David Hume explained away this void of logic. He illustrated the incorrectness of simply assuming that whatever *is* the case also *ought to be* the case. Using what is referred to by some as "Hume's Guillotine" for severing facts from values, we can slice and dice the Dahmer-esque illogic. Just because we did evolve in no way suggests that we ought to kill each other. Because natural selection works by way of "survival of the fittest," this fact does not require or even allow that the more "fit" *ought* to kill off the rest. Imagine applying the Stein-Dahmer thesis to gravity: It *is* the case that things fall toward the earth. So, therefore, we *should* never attempt to flee from the earth by way of airplane nor should we even jump, but should instead walk on *terra firma,* and crawl even, or if you are truly a devout naturalist, slink around on your belly. Children could provide this same sort of defense when scolded by their parents to clean their room: "But the thermodynamic law of entropy holds that everything tends toward disorder. Cleaning my room completely violates this law of nature!"

It seems that we could dissolve most—dare we say *all*—of the concerns of this bumper-sticker wisdom with a quick return to our practice of labeling. A shift from *theism* (belief in an active god who directs us and acts on the universe) to *deism* (belief in some higher power not involved with running the universe) dissolves all the harm done to adherents and their neighbors alike. And harm is really what we want to avoid so that we can all get on with loving our neighbors in the first place.

So no need to keep the killing scorecard updated anymore. It's clear that scientists and nature don't cause murder. And in order to continue valuing such unnatural virtues as turning the other cheek, monogamy, and the Golden Rule, we must realize that "natural" doesn't necessitate "good," nor does "good" necessitate "natural." And thus, Steven Pinker cites Katharine Hepburn's remark to Humphrey Bogart in *The African Queen*: "Nature, Mr. Allnut, is what we are put in this world to rise above."

KNOWLEDGE
What You Don't Know *Can* Hurt You

DON'T BELIEVE EVERYTHING YOU THINK

This bumper-sticker wisdom uses the word "think" in a softer way, serving the same function that "believe" often does as in, "Sorry, Officer, I *thought* I was going slower," or, "Sorry I'm late, I *thought* we were meeting at noon instead." Perhaps this bumper sticker should say, "Don't *Mindlessly* Believe Everything You Think." Or even just, "Think." IBM founder Thomas Watson used this one word—*Think*—as the company's primary slogan in its early years, having every employee display a placard with the word on their desks. Actually, flipping this bumper sticker on its head would really do it: "Think About Everything You Believe." Because when you really *think* about something, it's usually pretty easy to decipher: Think to check your speedometer instead of "thinking," or think to look at your calendar instead of going on a hunch.

As it turns out, a major portion of our thinking involves the emotional component of the brain. As any high school calculus teacher can tell you, if students are emotionally detached from what they're trying to learn, their eyes glaze over and they fail to connect. So they're likely not *thinking* too hard in the process. In the 1950s psychologist Jean Piaget suggested this connection between emotion and learning, which has been greatly advanced with the advent of neuroscience. As we find fifty years later, very often the "emotional rudder" helps steer rational thought and, in many instances, triggers it, also making it an "emotional engine" of sorts.

Preceding Piaget, David Hume wrote that reason is the slave of the passions. Applying this to current research, psychologist Jonathan Haidt makes the analogy of our emotions as the dog, with rationality as the tail. So the notion that we *first* rationalize an ethical decision and *then* feel it is actually incorrect—the tail wagging the dog, as it were. It turns out that our emotion drives such decisions and only afterward do we "wag our rational tail" and invent a reason for it. Take the death penalty, for example. It's as though one might ponder, "Looks like I'm for the death penalty. Humph. I wonder why. Yeah, that's it. We gotta get back at the scum who did that. And plus, we shouldn't spend money on murderers sitting in prison when we could spend it on education." And when some know-it-all comes along and rationally discounts those reasons—the death penalty actually costs more than life in prison, and our penal system doesn't punish for the sake of revenge—then the person will often invent more reasons to match their emotional verdict, which also may be faulty.

We can apply Haidt's findings as evidence supporting the social taboo of talking about ethics, politics, or religion at the dinner table. Because these issues are all emotionally driven, a disagreement only ignites the passions, often leading to pigeonholing and name-calling. "Bleeding-heart Liberal!" "Heartless Conservative!" And then, in tandem, "You just don't get it." "Jinx." But according to Haidt, Republicans and Democrats disagree at a fundamental level couched in varying moral foundations. Liberals tend to view morality as based on more formal notions of rights and duties and how we should treat each other. Haidt aligns this with John Stuart Mill's *On Liberty*, in which Mill supports the notion of a contractual society where power over another can only be exercised "to prevent harm to others." Conservatives, on the other hand, view morality more as a vehicle by which the family unit (not just the individual) can prosper and can serve as a template for other components of society. So, along with the liberal focus on caring and fairness, the conservative moral lens includes in-group loyalty, respect for authority, and concepts of purity and sanctity as well.

So, just imagine two people with such differing lenses looking at the same issue—same-sex marriage, abortion, taxation— together over dinner. If you plan to attend a strongly bipartisan dinner party in the near future, you might want to read up on the weather, television gossip, and local sports teams—unless you're prepared for a lot of dog-eat-dog irrational tail-wagging, and you don't plan on being invited back. But when you leave that setting, with discussing social justice and serious moral issues no longer on the line, you might want to try out another bumper-sticker prescription as well:

WAG MORE: BARK LESS

It seems to be working for our four-legged best friends.

WHEN I AM RIGHT NOBODY REMEMBERS. WHEN I AM WRONG NOBODY FORGETS!

Here's some good news/bad news all wrapped into one: Not to give you a complex, but you're probably wrong about this little hypothesis of yours. You just need a quick change in perspective and then you can go out and get yourself an "I am a good person" bumper sticker.

So you probably get stuck at all the red lights too, right? Always choose the longest line at the grocery store? You, like the rest of us, are also biased, and unfortunately, against yourself, like many of us. This "availability bias" causes you to remember the outstanding events. Who really remembers going through a green light— what's there to remember? Who remembers being right when you give someone the correct time or win a point for your trivia team? But sit at that red light, watching your second hand tick away for two minutes, and that's proof you're having a bad day. Oh, great, another red light. See, you really are having a bad day. And once this becomes the lens with which you view the world, you look for confirming instances all over, and you think, as you stand in that grocery store line watching the man in front argue that his beer was on sale for ten cents cheaper, "See, I knew it, I *am* having a bad day after all." As Sir Francis Bacon explained, once we "adopt an opinion," we seek to confirm it, even in light of there being more things that contradict it. Our brain "either does not notice them or rejects them, in order that this opinion will remain unshaken."

An email forward du jour recently surfaced based on just this "confirmation bias." The email directed readers to a webpage that instructed them to select a playing card from a lineup of six face cards. Upon doing this they were instructed to click the crystal ball and, during the moment when the screen goes blank, say the name of the chosen card out loud. When the cards re-appeared, the virtual magician made the subject's card disappear! Worked every time.

But all one needed to do was apply the antidote to confirmation bias—falsification: attempt to *dis*prove the crystal ball truths. Because in this case when the screen went blank, *all six* cards were exchanged for other face cards. But because the viewer focused only on his particular card and not the other five, when those changed they went unnoticed. We do tend to be a little myopic from time to time, and we confirm to a fault.

To make matters worse, you probably don't have a very firm grasp of statistics. Maybe not like Yogi Berra–bad—"Ninety percent of this game is half mental"—but bad nonetheless. How many randomly selected people need to be in a room before we should *expect* two of them to have the same birthday? When surveyed, people consistently intuit exceedingly high answers—something along the lines of: "Well, there are 365 days in a year, so about half of 365." Laying our intuition aside, simple mathematics yields the correct answer, twenty-three. When the room's population reaches a mere fifty, the chances rise to 97 percent that birthday buddies will be present. The key to our intuition gone awry lies in two factors. First, the problem becomes much clearer when we instead imagine the odds that two people in the room will *not* have the same birthday; and secondly, people often wrongly treat the question from their point of view: "What would the odds be that someone in the room has the same birthday as *me?*" which is an entirely different question. As Stanford University mathematician Persi Diaconis notes, your brain is "just not wired to do probability problems very well." So don't be so hard on yourself.

The real kicker comes when you sprinkle a little of nature's elixir into the equation, what physicist Leonard Mlodinow considers our "prime source of irrationality"—emotion. He compares our lives as akin to those of random swerving molecules, referred to by mathematicians as *the drunkard's walk*. The main difference is that, unlike atoms, we become emotional about our swerving and desperately want to assign meaning and order to it. Oftentimes you'd be better off actually drinking alcohol, getting drunk, and walking around—at least you'd have an explanation for it.

Imagine you are celebrating your fortieth birthday and your friend brings a bottle of BLS champagne. These are the initials of your dearly departed grandfather, Rob "Bob" Luis Stevenson, and so you assign order to that—"He must be here in this room," or "He's sending me a message." But you forget about all of the misses: all of the previous parties, dinners, get-togethers, celebrations, and holidays with no sign of him, or anyone dear to you. You also ignore all of the chances this could have occurred in various different ways, as you have ten departed relatives and friends, pets, etc., all with different initials, nicknames, pet names. You get the idea. So you likely realize—now that the emotion-buzz has worn off and you're thinking clearly—that you're kind of surprised this hasn't happened already. It was as though you'd thrown the dart first, and *then* painted the circle around it. Bull's-eye. Pass the champagne. Your grandfather probably really loved you.

Now that you have adhered to that cornerstone of stoicism, "Follow where reason leads," you can use this *for* yourself, instead of against. Pour a glass of champagne or two, go for a walk, and try flipping your bumper-sticker hypothesis on its head and paying attention to how often you're right. I bet you'll find that you were wrong after all.

MILITANT AGNOSTIC: I DON'T KNOW AND YOU DON'T EITHER

Agnostic. *A*—"without." *Gnōsis*—from the Greek, "knowledge." (Not to be confused with a-gnocchi: to be without the tasty Italian dish gnocchi.) Originally coined in 1869 by biologist Thomas "Darwin's Bulldog" Huxley, who advised, "Do not pretend that conclusions are certain which are not demonstrated or demonstrable." In other words, don't say you know something that can't be known. Quite militant of him, really.

An underlying confusion hovers around this term. It might be easier to altogether eliminate the label "agnostic" and instead, when someone asks "Do you believe in God?" the respondent can just say, "I dunno." That's essentially what they are saying in using this term. If we really need the labels, then theists and atheists should, for the time being, insert "agnostic" before their respective labels just to be clear about it all. Because *no one* knows if a supernatural being exists.

In this (weak) sense, we are all agnostic—i.e., lack *certainty*—about most of the things we purport to know. One claims to know where his car is parked, but clearly he could have forgotten, or it could have been stolen, borrowed by his spouse, etc. Yet even given all of that, he is not "without knowledge" of his car's position, as it's fair to say he still knows this little tidbit. So either knowledge requires absolute certainty and thus we actually have very little of it, or, more likely, it does not, in which case we're not really agnostic about as much as we claim to be. Weathermen, on the other hand, tend to apply more discretion. They never inform us, "We *know* it's going to rain tomorrow," but instead say, "Ninety-percent chance of showers for tomorrow." In other words, they *believe* it will rain, and for good reason too, with all their fancy equipment for detecting imminent rain. On those dark and cloudy mornings, they are "rainists," unlike in the summertime, when they tend to be more "*a*-rainist." Regardless, their beliefs don't require absolute certainty and that knowledge stuff may not require absolute certainty after all.

Agnosticism has two basic forms. The first: "I don't know *yet* but could eventually," as is the case for the 83 percent of young American adults surveyed by *National Geographic* who could not find Afghanistan on a map even after the war. (So much for that bumper-sticker wisdom "War Is God's Way of Teaching Americans Geography.") While one may not know the location of Afghanistan now, one *could* know. The second form, and in our case, "militant": "I don't know and can *never* know." Many hold this position regarding belief in supernatural beings such as god, though it can also be applied to other topics such as invisible fairies, the afterlife, and Elvis. Do you truly know if invisible fairies exist or not? We wouldn't judge an a-fairyist for claiming knowledge where they should not. And along those lines Sam Harris notes, " 'Atheism' is a term that should not even exist. No one ever needs to identify himself as a 'non-astrologer' or a 'non-alchemist.' "

Regarding theology, agnosticism often serves as a sort of "safe house" or midway point between theism (belief in a god) and atheism (no belief in a god, or its stronger form, a belief that no god exists). It's a gentle way of telling your god-worshiping friends that you think they're wrong while avoiding the use of the term "atheist." As a 2009 Pew Forum survey shows, only a quarter of people who describe themselves as "Do not believe in God" also consider themselves "atheist," even though each signifies the same thing. Clearly some social stigma comes with these labels. But there is an important difference. Agnosticism concerns *knowledge,* while theism and atheism deal with *belief.* "Militant agnosticism" is a position based on what it means to know something, holding that one must be more certain than she is now in order to make that claim. The bumper-sticker wisdom here—*super* militant agnosticism—just applies that position to everyone else. It's as if this sticker owner got her degree in epistemology (the study of knowledge), and she is telling everyone what she discovered on their behalf.

Plato developed three criteria for determining when a claim can be considered knowledge: (a) It must be *justified;* (b) It must be *true;* (c) We must *believe* it. How do you know you're holding this book? According to Plato: (a) You're wide-awake in good lighting, feeling and seeing it; (b) You *are* holding this book; (c) You believe you are (don't you?). Justified True Belief determines knowledge, and belief is just one component of that. Militant agnostics call into question "a": Not only they, but *you*, cannot *justify* making such a knowledge claim about supernatural beings. Theism and atheism involve just one component of knowledge: belief. If backed into a corner and forced by some inquisitor to pigeonhole yourself regarding supernatural beings, remember that no one *knows*. They're probably just asking you what you believe.

So agnosticism is not a safe house. If the church's Inquisition comes knocking at your door asking, "Do you believe in God?" and you respond, "I dunno," then don't expect them to treat you much differently than they did witches—you can't believe in something you don't even know about. To believe without knowing about why you believe is just atheism of the having-no-belief sort, kind of like every cute little newborn atheist baby.

Philosopher William James has us imagine a man standing atop a snowy mountain, uncertain whether to risk descending and perishing in an avalanche or to wait it out but risk freezing to death. Not deciding, though, doesn't alleviate the problem, unless he finds some comfort thinking to himself during his final moments atop Mount Indecision, "Well, I didn't choose this." For James, belief in god presents a similar "forced" situation—not believing is, well, not believing. And not believing is called atheism.

Likely, when a so-called agnostic closes his eyes and asks, "Are there invisible fairies or supernatural beings?" he gets an answer—

a *belief*. And quite often it is these beliefs that drive our actions in the first place. It makes one wonder: With agnostic atheists and agnostic theists, could one be an agnostic agnostic—is there room for that in the safe house?

"Are you an agnostic?"

"I dunno."

Sure you do.

THE LESS YOU KNOW THE MORE YOU BELIEVE

Certainly seems believable. Let's turn to some of our less knowledgeable humans to help shed light on this bumper-sticker wisdom:

"Mommy stops existing when she leaves the room," the average seven-month-old believes. This makes peek-a-boo especially fun for them (and us) and bolsters their belief that they can hide by merely closing their eyes: Out of sight, out of mind. "When do we start getting smaller?" the four-year-old asks her dad immediately following take-off (actual question), remembering all those airplanes she had previously seen shrinking off into the sky. "As soon as the lights go out, the creatures come to life in my room," says the five-year-old. "Santa fits down our chimney and 2 billion others all in the same night—though he sure seems to like Jimmie down the street more than me."

Eventually, knowledge becomes the antidote for these beliefs, or, for a more positive spin, a *pro*-dote (which would be Latin for "given for" if it were really a word). Unfortunately, Mommy and Daddy are up to similar shenanigans:

In 2006, Mommy gave half of her bank account to a New York psychic to remove a curse on her and her two children. In 2001, 41 percent of Mommies and Daddies believed that the actual Devil had inhabited them at some point. Last year thirteen died when a

Congo soccer goalkeeper yelled out spells against the other team, causing a riot. And quackery (pseudo-medicine, not as some might believe, the study of duck language) not only kills more than all violent crimes together, but Mommy and Daddy spend billions on it every year.

Clearly something is going wrong, for if Mommy *knew* that astrology didn't work, or that yelling words at someone wouldn't turn them into a newt, her family would certainly be better off. It turns out we're all little belief-machines, because believing is important for us to even act. The question is, what to believe and how to get our paws on some of that knowledge-stuff.

Philosopher William Clifford famously addressed just this issue. He argued not only that we should refrain from acting on an ill-founded belief, but also that it would be immoral to do so. We can take a current example similar to one he gives: In 2007, a Nepal Airlines Boeing 757 experienced technical problems before takeoff so they sacrificed two goats to appease the Hindu sky god. Clifford writes of such a decision arguing that they had "no right to believe on such evidence" regarding killing goats and their relation to airplane safety. His concern being that they had acquired their belief "not by honestly earning it in patient investigation, but by stifling [their] doubts." He reminds us that no belief is a merely private matter—i.e., they involve plane passengers, our children, etc.—and that, worse, we can come to develop the habit of relying on ill-founded beliefs and then "sink back into savagery." As he was writing in 1890, it seems like we should categorize him more as a prophet rather than a philosopher.

This may seem a bit strong, but probably not so much in light of such travesties as the 1997 Heaven's Gate UFO cult that committed mass suicide or the less extreme groups claiming Elvis has not left the building. What might Clifford say about the CIA's spending $20 million on "remote viewing" in which the "viewer" sits in Washington, D.C., closes his eyes, and "looks" for those infamous WMDs across the globe—no wonder we never found them, or did we (another nod to "Military Intelligence")? Clifford would have been quite taken by Voltaire, who wrote, "Those who can make you believe absurdities can make you commit atrocities." Someone should get that on a bumper sticker. And he would have been quite in line with modern-day philosopher Sam Harris, who observes, "I know of no society in human history that ever suffered because its people became too desirous of evidence in support of their core beliefs."

But getting knowledge takes effort. Think back to all those hours spent in school, doing homework, trying to distinguish truth from falsity. Take the story of Noah's Ark. Sixty percent of Mommies and Daddies reportedly believe this story to be literally true (that itself is hard to believe, until you also discover that a third believe aliens have visited earth). So, either, (a) After celebrating his six hundredth birthday, a man and his kids built a boat big enough to hold 2 million animal species, with everything from dinosaurs to insects, and then set sail with seven other people; or, (b) Someone invented this story to scare people into believing him, which would explain why only animals known to his demographic were included, the fossil record doesn't match up, there's no mention of microorganisms, etc. Even today, a recently appointed Vatican bishop claims that, just like Noah's flood, the recent Hurricane Katrina was "divine retribution" for their community's tolerance of homosexuals. This destructive belief is squelched with knowledge—the *least* affected areas in the flood zone were those with the highest population density of homosexuals. Either this super-perfect god missed his mark, or Clifford's whole "wrong beliefs cause savagery" idea was right.

So now you know, or so they say.

> # EVOLUTION IS A FACT.
> # GOD IS JUST A THEORY.

Not quite. But on the right track. Let's clear up this fact-theory dichotomy once and for all.

You come home from the movies with your ten-year-old cousin and his three friends. You all walk into the kitchen to enjoy the cheese you had left out, only to discover that it has disappeared. Your cousin shakes his head and, smiling, says, "It looks like our Invisible Friend finally got something to eat. He hasn't eaten for days." The other three nod along, smiling. You furrow your eyebrows as you realize their sincerity, so you calmly say, "I have a theory." After you point out the rodent droppings on the counter near the empty cutting board and the tiny paw prints leading to a small crevice in the corner of the room, you suggest, "A mouse ate our cheese." Your cousin quickly responds, "But you didn't see it," which earns the support of three fervently head-nodding friends. He continues, "And don't try to tell me I'm wrong by using your funny-talk. You can't prove that I'm wrong, and all of us think I'm right." The boys smile in unison, and then, as if having delivered the final knock-down argument in a John Grisham court case, he proclaims, "Yours is *only a theory* anyway."

"Theory" is often used synonymously with "wacky guess," typically regarding events that no one saw and that no one can prove are *absolutely* right. But a scientific theory is really just a strongly supported hypothesis. For example, the *theory* of gravity has been repeatedly confirmed and you can test it yourself. Imagine criticizing it as "just a theory," and that all high school physics textbooks had multiple warning labels similar to that suggested for evolution by creationists, such as this parody by physicist Ellery Schempp: "This textbook contains material on Gravity. Universal gravity is a theory, not a fact, regarding the natural law of attraction." For that matter, every single proposition in all science textbooks would require similar "theory heckles," including the theories that the spherical earth revolves around the sun, that antigens cause sneezing (not demons, as we once thought), and that electrons swirl around the nucleus.

So this bumper sticker is both right and wrong.

It's right in the sense that it uses the words "theory" and "fact" in the way that most people do, as if theory were a mere "hunch." In that case, it actually helps to frame the discussion. But it is wrong in the true sense that evolution *is* a theory—I'll leave out the "just a" caveat used by creationists as if to condemn it in the "wacky guess" formulation (the Wacky Guess of Gravitation). And it's supported by a mountain of evidence: thousands of scientist-reviewed journal articles, huge collections of fossils, carbon dating, DNA investigation and mapping, and the more recent opportunity to watch evolution in action as in the case of forced mating of Drosophila flies (with a ten-day life span we can observe evolution of many generations in a short time), selective breeding of dogs (where do you think all these breeds came from?), and the unfortunate case of the evolution of antibiotic-resistant strains of bacteria. As another bit of bumper-sticker wisdom pointedly asks (or, rather, *tells* through rhetoric),

I FORGET, WHICH DAY DID GOD CREATE ALL THE FOSSILS?

The concern of creationists regarding the fact that no one saw evolution "happen" misses the point entirely. Whoever was there to catalog God creating Adam and Eve *together* on the sixth day, it's hard to imagine. And in the very same book (Genesis) we learn that God created Adam first and only much later took one of Adam's ribs while he was napping and built Eve out of it. Two competing theories from the same book. This clearly seems to fall closer to the Wacky Guess end of the spectrum. A book proposal in today's publishing industry with inherent contradictions in the opening two chapters wouldn't make it through the first round of editing.

And the other non-scientific guesses aren't much better (actually, they're equal). Wikipedia's "Creation Myth" entry provides fifty-nine more "theories," including everything from the Christian God-Said-So theory to the Hindu's world-resulting-from-a-cosmic-egg theory to the Babylonian theory that the earth and skies result from the dismembering of the ocean goddess, Tiamat.

Yet the cleverness of all creation stories—and of invisible cheese-stealing friends—relies on the notion that no amount of testing or investigation could ever disprove them. And while extremely unlikely, in your most open-minded state maybe you can admit to the very slight chance that your cousin surmised correctly.

FORGET ABOUT ARTIFICIAL INTELLIGENCE, LET'S FIX NATURAL STUPIDITY

We have created robots that can do everything from proving previously unproven theorems to mopping our entire home while we're at work. But we have yet to build a robot that can perform such tasks as those cataloged in the bestselling *Darwin Awards,* in which naturally stupid humans remove themselves from the gene pool by doing things like jumping out of planes to film skydivers without a parachute, or opening a mail bomb they themselves sent but which was returned to them for lacking postage. So much for "Ignorance is bliss." So why all the fuss? Can we really get robots to be as "intelligent" *as* we are? Intelligent *like* we are?

The cover of a 1950 *Time* magazine featured a human-like robot with the text "Can man build a superman?" and a cover story entitled, "The Thinking Machine." In it, they even worried that computers might eventually think so hard that they develop psychoses and require treatment such as rest (being shut down), shock therapy (increased voltage), and lobotomies (removal of parts). We certainly need to be careful of anthropomorphizing anything simply because it *acts* human. Then again, Pet Rocks, the 1970s fad—rocks with eyes glued to them—had sales of over a million dollars and included a training manual with instructions on how to get the rock to "sit" and "stay." Good rock. Good computer.

But before computer scientists can even get to work on computer-achieved thought and intelligence, philosophers weigh in to help determine just how to know how we would accomplish the feat in the first place. We can't have the inventor of the thermostat claiming that your thermostat actually *thinks* when it "decides" to heat the house. It's like they've set the game but don't know how to determine if they win. Just what is thinking and intelligence?

One such attempt, known as the Turing Test, requires that the entity in question—in this case, a computer—can converse in a human-like manner. The experimenter engages in a text-only conversation with a human and a computer. If he cannot distinguish between the two, then Turing argued the computer has achieved thought. Basically, if it acts like a duck, walks like a duck, quacks like a duck, then it's a duck. Armed with this information, we're now in the 1 percent who can understand this additional bumper-sticker wisdom from a fellow human:

I FAILED THE TURING TEST

This bumper-sticker owner is clearly not happy with the Turing Test as a method for discovering thought—either that or he's really not much of a conversationalist and probably not invited back to many cocktail parties. But take a moment to reflect on how *you* determine that another person *thinks:* You spend time with your family, friends, cohorts, and after a few interactions, they sure *behave* as though they think, so you assume they think. Your own little Turing Test. And steer clear of anyone who fails it and then announces it on their bumper—sounds more like some sort of android.

The real concern becomes just what to do with the exponentially increasing computer technology. Despite the engineer who won the award for Cynic of the Century when he asked of the microchip in 1968, "But what is it good for?" we have found myriad uses. So many so that it looks like Frank Lloyd Wright might have been unfortunately prophetic as he warned, "If it keeps up, man will atrophy all his limbs but the push-button finger." We are a pet-stone's-throw away from creating "virtual" experiences, the primary one, it seems, being the opportunity to be intimate with any popular icon of one's choosing. If a married man spends the afternoon with Virtual Pam, has he cheated? And a recent story tells of a man who spends hours in a virtual game world, in which he is married to a virtual woman (also played by a real-life woman) in a game-town with whom he has virtual children, argues, makes love, goes to the movies—all within the game. His real-life wife is upset because he takes out the trash in the game and gets points for it, but still won't do it at home. Maybe life is a game after all. Now at least we have found an answer to the word-eating Digital Equipment Corporation founder's comment in 1977, "There is no reason anyone would want a computer in their home."

It does seem as though we've become reliant on, and even addicted to, computers, as only one other class of substance elicits the term "users" to reference its participants. So maybe we could just invent a computer to tell us if computers could ever think. Would that be so stupid?

SUBVERT THE DOMINANT PARADIGM

Paradigm—the collective perspective of an entire community.

So this bumper sticker could also read, "Abolish the Popular Way of Thinking and Worldview," or, for our younger readers, "Make Everyone Stop Thinking the Way They're Thinking."

With a majority of these bumper stickers likely sold to owners of Volkswagen buses circa 1960, by definition these sticker owners are the counterculture rebels, typically in the minority. If they were in the majority then they'd *be* the dominant paradigm and more interested in its upkeep than its subversion.

As with many catchy phrases, this imparts a helpful bit of wisdom. Thank goodness for this bumper-sticker wisdom applied by Copernicus, Galileo, et al., as they subverted the dominant paradigm at the time which placed the earth at the center of the universe. And kudos to whomever may have placed this sticker on their wagon, urging abolitionists such as Lincoln and the aptly named Sojourner Truth to contest the then-dominant paradigm of slavery.

But hopefully we won't have people mindlessly following this bumper-sticker wisdom today, subverting the already-subverted paradigm, thus reverting back to slavery. And to apply this to current paradigms and ethical mores like quantum physics and abortion, it would seem odd to simply survey the "world of viewers" and then just adopt the *contrary* position, as the bumper sticker suggests. And what if "subverting the dominant paradigm" *is* the dominant paradigm? Time to print a new bumper sticker. Clearly, logical and practical problems arise if one truly embraces this slogan.

Philosopher G. K. Chesterton summarizes the problem nicely. He refers to our paradigm-subverter as "The modern man in revolt," and explains that he has "become practically useless for all purposes of revolt. By rebelling against everything he has lost his right to rebel against anything." Thinking outside of the box has led to some of our most valued discoveries in humanity's moral and scientific lives, such as the theory of relativity, penicillin, the eradication of slavery, and the Slinky. But mindlessly emptying the box and subverting all box-worthy tidbits of knowledge and values makes for a nearly impossible, even empty, way of life.

The term "paradigm" became popularized in 1962 by philosopher Thomas Kuhn in reference to a particular culture's common, agreed-upon views held by scientists, which then frame their work from that point on. Kuhn's thesis implicitly highlighted a virtue of this bumper-sticker wisdom and a practical application in one's own life. As we become committed to a particular worldview, we frame all of our experiences through that lens and, in a sense, entrench ourselves deeper in that paradigm. Were we to live in the time of the geocentric paradigm, as we awoke to the dawn of a new day, we would literally see the sun *rise* up over the horizon—a "sun *rise*" as they say. Our paradigm not only frames what we see, but directs the questions we ask and how we answer them.

Kuhn warned of the difficulty in shifting paradigms. As we become so psychologically tied to one view, we need to be seriously shaken even to be open to such change as we literally fail to *see* anything else. Imagine what the deeply religious person would have to undergo to cease seeing God in every object and action, or the deeply committed atheist to find "evidence" for such supernatural activity. So, maybe while we are "inside the box," living out the dominant paradigm, we can take a more realistic approach. Instead of "Subvert," maybe it should command, "Question," or "Reexamine," or at least "Be Consciously Aware of" the dominant paradigm. And we can think of what might be outside of our own box, but not throw the box out with the bathwater.

ETHICS
Two Rights Make a Right

AT LEAST THE WAR ON THE ENVIRONMENT IS GOING WELL

So we know a few things about this sticker owner: He thinks the recent war the U.S. intentionally entered is going poorly; he has a somewhat witty and sarcastic disposition; and he not only agrees with the data showing a steady increase in global temperature and depletion in ecosystems but also the idea that humans have directly affected these fluctuations. But if we do actually finish and "win" the war on the environment, there will be no one around to proclaim "Mission Accomplished," so it's worth looking into what exactly is going on in our environmental battle.

Initially, it all seemed quite clear: Al Gore made a film, showed a few polar bears dying, and gave everyone a new cause to support. But Gore's film, *An Inconvenient Truth,* did more than display a few bits of anecdotal evidence—because you can find anecdotes to support any wacky hypothesis. Gore presented *data*. Statistics. Scientific research. The kind of stuff that polar bear aficionados hate to deal with that, in the end, yields that ever-so-elusive "truth" that can often be so darned inconvenient.

With every campaign for truth come the conspiracy theorists who have cried "hoax" for everything from the moon landing, to the Holocaust, to the JFK assassination, to the government actually plotting and planning the 9/11 tragedy. Our John Grisham–trained ears perk up and we ask: What would motivate such a massive conspiracy? Why would the former Vice President, the United Nations, National Resources Defense Council, National Academy of Sciences, and on and on fabricate a story about the impending doom of our planet? Because aside from those who actually want the end-times, Armageddon-style end of the world, people really do seem to like living on this planet.

The subtitle of Chris Horner's book *Red Hot Lies* answers it best: *How Global Warming Alarmists Use Threats, Fraud, and Deception to Keep You Misinformed.* Here's the supposed motivation: The global warming lobby wants Americans living in fear because this fear results in more government and thus more power and more control. In addition, scientists who have families to feed and new gadgets to purchase have the added conflicting interest of creating interest so they can earn grants to do their work. It all starts to sound fishy until you also discover that Horner serves as a senior fellow for the conservative think tank Competitive Enterprise Institute, whose major funders include those leading the wars: Exxon Mobil, Texaco, Ford, General Motors, and numerous other corporations.

Aside from all of the finger-pointing and motive-searching, we do have facts coming in. The National Resources Defense Council lays out a simple explanation of the global crisis. Carbon dioxide traps heat in the atmosphere. This raises the temperature, causing ice to melt and sea levels to rise, resulting in myriad other problems. It also results in excessive heat waves, droughts, and fires. And humans are producing more carbon dioxide than ever.

Scientific American columnist Michael Shermer explains his conversion from skepticism about environmental warming to his newfound activism in the face of the data. Much like Goldilocks settling on a bear's home that was "just right," with the other two being too extreme on opposite ends of the spectrum, the earth is similarly picky. Known as the Goldilocks Principle: On the one extreme, during the Ice Age there was too little carbon dioxide (180 parts per million) and thus no life could flourish; then the earth warmed as we arrived at the Industrial Revolution, settling in at a cozy 280—"Just right." Currently, we're at about 380 and rising. It is projected that in the next hundred years, we'll arrive at upwards of 550, and this is just too much for any Goldilocks to live.

There is no question that humans contribute to this, it's just a question of how much. In our Hummer-driving, Styrofoam-using, overconsuming way of life, are we spitting into the ocean of naturally occurring greenhouse gasses or, as the data shows, creating oceans of it ourselves? Planets warm and cool in cycles, just as the once-planet Pluto has also warmed even during the time that its orbit took it farther from the sun.

Until recently many moral theories valued the human being over all else, including the promotion by caveat in Genesis bestowing humans "dominion over all the earth." But with the onset of environmental ethics, more holistic approaches emerged with everything from the Gaia Hypothesis—viewing the earth as a self-sustaining entity *à la* "Mother Earth"—to Deep Ecology, in which the environment as a whole earns the moral consideration once given solely to humans. Champion of the Gaia Hypothesis James Lovelock recently suggested that "global warming" is not occurring. Instead he offers a more accurate phrase that he hopes will jolt citizens a bit more: "global heating"—because no one cares too much about just being warm.

Environmental philosophers force us to consider whether the earth and its ecosystem has some intrinsic value, or just an "instrumental" value in which we need the earth to function properly so we can do our thing. For example, do we give value to a tree because of the wood, shade, paper, and beauty that it provides *us,* or do we value it *for its own sake?* Or maybe both, as we might value a doctor? If you have concern about saving a particular species of animal, is it for the animal's sake (intrinsic) or yours, because you like seeing or eating them (instrumental)? If there is intrinsic value, then it does seem that it should acquire a moral status greater than that of other purely instrumentally valuable things. You can ask yourself just what motivates your own interest in preventing any species' extinction.

All of this forces a discussion of duties, namely a duty to future generations. Clearly, parents have a duty to provide for children and even grandchildren. But what of really really "grand" children one thousand years down the road? The Great Law of the Iroquois Indians demands that "In every deliberation, we must consider the impact of the seventh generation"—the *super-duper* grandchildren. And what of those unrelated neighbors across the globe? Considered the founder of Deep Ecology, Arne Næss described all organisms as "knots" in the connected biosphere. He emphasized the ripple effects that our actions have, and that those who act without knowledge of the ensuing ripples ought not act at all. He stressed that we are not just individuals—"No man is an island entire unto himself," as poet John Donne wrote—but that our true Self is an integral part of something much greater.

Regardless of one's belief in the data, the Self, and the value of the planet, what real motivation is there to continue fighting *against* instead of *for* the planet? As the parent nags the child to "Clean your room," shouldn't we do the same as adults in our shared Room? For, to push the analogy one step further, the nagging parent could threaten, ". . . or I will lock you out." And there's no way to put the typical response lightly in terms of this analogy: "But where will I live?" So if you can't love Pluto, maybe you can at least

LOVE YOUR MOTHER 🌏

THE MOST DANGEROUS PLACE TO BE IS . . . IN A MOTHER'S WOMB!

Sounds scary. I'd hate to ever be in one of those. Oh, wait . . .

First, let's be clear about the message: Because we allow abortions and then so many people have them, while we may think *our* world is dangerous (war, disease, drunk drivers, swine flu, and so on), it turns out that being an embryo is even more hazardous, and since we don't want danger in our lives, we shouldn't allow it for the lives of embryos.

What this bumper sticker says is true—more true than the sticker-placing embryo-lover likely knows. Though before they superglue the sticker to their bumper, they should allow the following bit of biology to gestate in their mental womb before giving birth to an unwanted idea.

The amazingly complex process of human birth requires thousands of things to be just so for the pregnancy to progress to the point at which the woman even knows she's pregnant. Because of this, of every 100 eggs that are fertilized (sperm meets egg) only 33 continue naturally to a full-term pregnancy—51 fail to implant in the uterus and 16 naturally abort due to imperfect conditions.

In the United States there were nearly 6 million *known* pregnancies in 2008. Approximately 1.3 million of these were terminated intentionally, though if we extrapolate the numbers from the above discussion, an estimated 4 million embryos died naturally—that's three times the number of human-induced abortions.

One may argue, "Yes, but this is nature running its course." Yet, when "nature runs its course" in our lives, we intervene with antibiotics, surgery, chemotherapy, and so on. And where we cannot intervene we have scientists working on it, as in the case of AIDS and Alzheimer's. The concern for our bumper-sticker wisdom is: A mother's womb *is* a dangerous place—each year 4 million embryos don't live through the first two weeks. Yet, the "life begins at conception" faction spends not a moment on those, and focuses on the remaining 1.3 million. With so many "innocent citizens" dying, we would expect some think tank, foundation, or major grant program to spring up to attempt to prevent these deaths, yet no such thing exists. Instead we focus on considerably lesser killers such as heart disease, cancer, and Alzheimer's (which claim a combined 1.3 million lives per year). And we are right to focus on those. Given that actions speak louder than words, it looks like the sticker owner could stand to listen to their own actions—and non-actions—a bit.

CLONES ARE PEOPLE TOO

Finally an answer to poet William Blake's "Little Lamb, who made thee?"—Dr. Ian Wilmut did. And amid the scientific and philosophical seriousness of it all, the creator of the first cloned mammal had some semblance of a sense of humor. On July 5, 1996, "Dolly" was born as a result of cloning the mammary cell of a sheep and thus given the namesake of the buxom country singer Dolly Parton. This opened the real possibility of cloning a human being.

As for this bumper-sticker wisdom, though, one wonders just who would disagree? We might imagine that in frighteningly recent history bumper stickers replacing "Clones" with the word "Blacks," "Women," or "Jews" would not have been universally well received. While everyone would agree that all four categories mentioned here are *human* (i.e., they have human DNA), the question at hand is, "Are they people?" A brief understanding of the facts helps to inform the investigation. To bluntly foreshadow, the answer to all of the above is a resounding "Yes."

In the tersest of all biology lessons, a human *clone* (derived from the Greek "twig") is a human created from the DNA of *one* human versus our standard Make-Love-Not-War version of sperm and egg. And they already exist—identical twins are essentially clones of each other, as they result from the same set of DNA. Cut from the same mold. With cloning, the "parent" would be directly related to the clone as a "blood-sibling."

Once the initial science-fiction fears give way to a little knowledge, the answer becomes pretty simple. Clones really are people, just like identical twins are people. And the practice confers many benefits: another reproductive choice for infertile individuals, avoiding transmission of genetic disease between generations, "replacement" of a deceased loved one, creation of organ donors, and of course, the science-fiction fear of creating entire clone armies to make war while we're busy making love the old-fashioned way.

A brief review of the literature reveals the most referenced clone-to-be as Michael Jordan. "Do we really want a bunch of Jordans walking around?" commentators rhetorically ask. The interest in the future of humanity's ability to throw a ball through a circle notwithstanding, we can frame the problems nicely through this lens. In 2002, the President's Council on Bioethics released their report recommending a ban on cloning to produce children and a four-year moratorium on cloning for biomedical research. Their anticipated concerns are briefly summarized here through our Jordan-lens:

1. Identity—Jordan has already lived, so Jordan-2 will live a life that has "already lived" and that's not fun for clones.

2. Commercialization—People will become viewed as products and we won't value all the new Jordans intrinsically as we did the original. Also, Jordans 2 through 12 will form an unstoppable basketball team.

3. Eugenics—We will choose certain features (jumping) over others, thus creating unnatural value.

4. Family Relations—Jordan will be Jordan-2's father *and* brother and then eventually Jordan-3's grandfather and father and brother, *ad infinitum.* Jordan won't know whether to mentor, tease, or tell stories of "Back in the Day," for all ensuing Jordans.

From our brief lesson in cloning we realize that many of these concerns are ill-founded, just as identical twins don't experience extraordinary angst nor cause unease for the public at large. A real concern noted by the chairman of the Bioethics Council, ethicist Leon Kass, is the harm done to "failed" clones—nearly all biologists predict that en route to perfecting the technique, many people will be created with severe deformities. Another overarching worry is couched in that nebulous term "Playing God." Kass writes that placing "the origin of human life literally in human hands" has led "to the continuing erosion of respect for the mystery of sexuality and human renewal."

Regardless of sex being mysterious for some or humdrum for others, it turns out that human clones truly are (well, *will be*) people. As is often the case, simple bumper-sticker wisdom provides the opportunity for deep reflection, and another chance to more closely explore our own humanity.

PETA: PEOPLE EATING TASTY ANIMALS

If you're not up to speed on your animal politics then you likely find this announcement strange: Why are you sharing what you had for dinner and how tasty it was? There's a group for everyone, and this one exists to support our meat-eating, fur-wearing, animal-hunting human animal friends. Everyone needs to belong to something.

They stole the catchy acronym from another, more active group, PETA—People for the Ethical Treatment of Animals. They literally stole the name, as determined by a court of law (*PETA v. PETA*) in which Tasty-PETA eventually had to surrender the domain name peta.org to Ethical-PETA on grounds of cybersquatting (actual term). It looks like, when making websites, ethical animal-treaters stand while meat-eaters cybersquat.

Who could have a problem with PETA and treating animals ethically? While they do many good things, and bring to light copious injustices, they also bark up the wrong tree a bit, which, unfortunately, meat eaters and powerful corporations bring into the public eye.

The methods of PETA are certainly questionable at times. As

one PETA spokesman states, "Of course we're going to be blowing things up and smashing windows" in order to maintain the rights of animals, whom they view as moral equals. This explains their placing a dead raccoon on the dining table of *Vogue* editor Anna Wintour in protest of her support of fur. Looks like the devil wears fur, too. With the horrors of the fur trade invisible to many, PETA's campaign intends to bring to light the methods used, such as live skinning and holding animals captive in small cages for their entire lives before slowly killing them to protect their fur. It's hard to imagine how people can support Tasty-PETA's pro-fur stance once they learn the facts.

Taking a different tack, PETA-sponsored supermodels Christy Turlington and Kim Basinger posed on billboards as naked as jaybirds to protest wearing fur, with the byline "I'd rather go naked than wear fur." It's hard to determine just who that dissuades. One can imagine their continued threats to Americans: "And if you keep wearing fur, then we will collect all of the super-duper models and make you look at them naked!" (They dressed Martha Stewart in a button-down shirt for her exposé.)

In a nice bit of irony, Pam Anderson's car auctioned to benefit PETA had leather seats, and Jenna Jameson was photographed eating oysters, fishing, and wearing a leather jacket just days after her anti-leather PETA-sponsored campaign launched. Seems fishy. (Note to self: Don't hire porn stars for ethics campaign.) Then, following a 2003 terrorist bombing in Jerusalem, PETA was understandably distraught. They wrote a letter to PLO leader Yasser Arafat asking that, in future terrorist acts, they not use animals as they did in this case, in which a donkey carried the explosives. Donkeys get all the harms (being blown up) and none of the spoils (no heaven of virgin donkeys).

PETA president Ingrid Newkirk launched a "Holocaust on Your Plate" campaign to compare the slaughter of animals to the treatment of Jews in the Holocaust. Many considered this tasteless and offensive to Jews and relatives of Holocaust victims. Though as philosopher Isaac Bashevis Singer wrote, "In relation to [animals], all people are Nazis; for the animals it is an eternal [Nazi prison camp]." It looks like the phrase "A dog's life" turns out to be the case mostly just for dogs.

PETA does great work in many other arenas, bringing to public attention the horrendous, stomach-turning treatment of animals by such corporations as McDonald's, Kentucky Fried Chicken, and Armani, and other institutions such as circuses. They highlight the severe injustices done through such practices as the violent force-feeding of ducks for foie gras, treatment of young calves to make veal, and the severe pain inflicted on animals by such cosmetic companies as Cover Girl in testing makeup on them. At the least, a boycott of these companies will clip the wings of such practices.

Granted, Newkirk and PETA have clearly embraced being the black sheep of the community, fighting an uphill battle in our man-eat-dog, meat-eating world. So she's likely to make an occasional overt statement, such as her defense of equal rights for all beings: "A rat is a pig is a dog is a boy." Regardless of whether you think a rat is a boy (morally speaking, of course), a little birdie's-eye view might encourage you not to throw the puppy out with the bathwater and give the bird to these industries; even go feed a bird with two biscuits instead of killing two with a stone. And remember, there's a chance that the Buddhists got it right and that if you fall prey to these traps of the "Tasty-PETA" sort, you yourself may come back as an animal, and you'll really look like the canary that the cat swallowed.

IF MEN COULD GET PREGNANT, ABORTION WOULD BE A SACRAMENT!

Starting at the very end of the sticker and working backward—does the bumper-sticker owner really need to yell this? Abortion stickers contain more exclamation points than any others, with gun control a distant second. Death penalty, euthanasia, even the pro/anti-religious fanatics all appear more subdued in their bumper-sticker communication. This is admittedly a touchy subject and one we should maybe address more calmly; thus the absence of exclamation points from here on out.

If anything, this sticker forces us to think outside of the box. As for abortion being a sacrament . . . The early Greek philosopher Augustine of Hippo defined "sacrament" as "a visible sign of an invisible reality." Sacraments include the most sacred affairs in a religion such as baptism, confirmation, and confession. For example, the invisible reality of confession is that God is actually on the other side of the partition and you're really telling Him that you accidentally worked last Saturday instead of resting, or that you just *thought* about coveting your neighbor's wife. It's hard to imagine what hidden reality would loom behind male abortion. Then again, given the high rate of divorce among Catholics, it's also hard to know what weight a sacrament even carries anymore.

The "If men could get pregnant" portion of this sticker would incite a field day for sociologists, psychologists, and social commentators. Feminist icon Gloria Steinem has come close in her anticipation of how society's view of menstruation might change in her article "If Men Could Menstruate": "Men would brag about how long and how much . . . Sanitary supplies would be federally funded and free. Of course, some men would still pay for the prestige of such commercial brands as Paul Newman Tampons, Muhammed Ali's Rope-a-Dope Pads," etc., etc.

She continues to surmise that religious fundamentalists would cite male-only menstruation as evidence that only men could do God's work—after all, it is called "*men*-struation"—in areas such as combat and political office, as well as high church positions. She is likely responding to the Bible's teaching that a menstruating woman is "unclean" during that time—as well as the seven days that follow—and if you touch said woman then you too become unclean (I truly wish I were making this up). In Steinem's sci-fi menstruating-men world she suggests that instead, menstruation would demonstrate that men alone should be priests, as God himself "gave his blood for our sins" and that the exclusively male rabbis' "monthly purge of impurities" would actually *purify* them, though of course they would still need to steer clear of the "unclean" women who would then lack such a divine biological gift.

Taking baby steps from here to the idea of male-only pregnancy, we can only imagine the changes in worldview, with men competing for longest labor (or would "quickest" become virtuous?) and the Bud Super-Light commercials for Beer Balancing On Pregnant Belly competitions highlighting the virtue of the Baby Beer Belly. Or maybe, as Steinem alludes, this bumper sticker is right, and abortions would become en vogue after all— the new notch on the bedpost.

In a defense of the pro-life position, philosopher Celia Wolf-Devine flips this bumper-sticker wisdom on its infantile, still-forming head. She argues that because the language of ethics is primarily couched in masculine ideals—such as contracts, power, and individualism—we all view abortion through that lens. She urges us to also consider the feminine perspectives of nurturance, care, and community in light of this and realize that the logic may lie outside of our current scope—outside of the box of paternalistic morality.

Steinem neatly summarizes both positions in a history-is-written-by-the-winners sort of way: "Logic is in the eye of the logician." In true bumper-sticker fashion, she is both right and wrong. Right, in the sense that the zeitgeist of public discourse takes orders from the party in power: in this case, men. But logic is logic (how's that for a logical truth)—if all bachelors are unmarried then no bachelors are married, regardless of who says it or thinks it. The stoics urge us that when in pursuit of the truth we should avoid the obstacles of emotion and passions: what they literally translated as "suffering." Maybe, though, following *pure logic* is just too strangely romantic of an ideal—and there's no room for romance in a discussion of male abortion! (Oops!)

I HAVE NO PROBLEM WITH EUTHANASIA. THE YOUTH IN ASIA MADE MY TENNIS SHOES.

An amazing two-issues-for-the-price-of-one bumper sticker, with mercy killing and sweatshops the most unlikely bedfellows. To hone the focus, we'll start with the first half of the sticker, examined through the lens of the following bumper-sticker wisdom:

"EUTHANASIA" IS AN OXYMORON. THERE'S NO SUCH THING AS A *GOOD DEATH.*

"Good death" derives from the Greek *eu* and *thanatos*. While we're breaking down the roots of words, "oxymoron" is itself an oxymoron borrowing from the Greek *oxy*—sharp—and *moros*—dull. Oxymorons, thus, transmit sharp-wittedness through seemingly dull statements. In this case, dying is bad, yet some believe it can be made good. How very sharp and dull.

Upon entering the medical profession, doctors take some form of the Hippocratic Oath to provide a foundation for their duties as a physician. Attributed to the Greek physician Hippocrates, circa 400 B.C., it includes the pledge "I will keep [patients] from harm." Yet in light of this "Do no harm" principle, doctors do *hurt* their patients repeatedly (and thankfully) in the form of sticking needles in their veins, performing surgery, and doing spinal taps—as those who have had one know, very few things hurt more. But "hurt" doesn't necessarily imply the deeper sense of "harm." An additional part of the oath helps to better align this, instructing doctors to refrain from "all intentional ill-doing" (it continues, prohibiting doctors the "pleasures of love" with their patients). Recently, some medical schools have updated the oath. The "Oath of Lasagna" (real name, taken from the name of its author, Louis Lasagna), aside from no longer obliging doctors to swear to Apollo and other Greek gods, includes, "It may also be within my power to take a life." It also requires the always-vague, "Above all, I must not play at God." Playing God involves even more shades of gray, as nearly everything a doctor does prevents something from happening that otherwise would have as God supposedly intended it. Medicine contributes greatly to our longer, healthier life span and it would be odd to accuse a doctor by saying "God gave me this cancer and then you took it away."

Currently, just 14 percent of medical schools in the U.S. and Canada forbid euthanasia (though only 3 percent explicitly disallow sexual contact with patients). So to more accurately examine euthanasia, it is important to understand the terms associated with euthanasia:

Voluntary: A terminally ill patient desires and consents to death.

Involuntary: A patient in what is commonly referred to as a persistent vegetative state (PVS) is killed.

Active: A doctor kills the patient, typically with an injection of morphine or ceasing a life-support system.

Passive: A doctor "lets" the patient die when he or she could otherwise prevent death.

Physician-assisted suicide: A patient carries out the final step as provided by their doctor, such as taking pills or flipping a switch; most contend that this does not constitute euthanasia.

Dr. Jack Kevorkian recently popularized voluntary, active euthanasia and physician-assisted suicide and claims to have helped 130 people through the process. This came to a halt in 1999 when he was convicted of second-degree homicide after filming his euthanizing of a patient with ALS who was unable to commit his own suicide. On the video he challenged the legal system to try stopping him from helping people like this, and so a judge declared, "Consider yourself stopped." In 2005, following seven years of legal controversy, the Terri Schiavo case brought involuntary euthanasia into the public eye. Terri was diagnosed as in a PVS, her feeding tubes were removed, and she subsequently died. Autopsy reports confirmed that her brain had, in fact, deteriorated to half of its original weight.

Active euthanasia remains considerably more controversial than passive, with advocates arguing that doctors who kill their patients differ not just in scope but in kind from doctors who simply allow their patients to die naturally. Ethicist James Rachels provides a thought experiment that attempts to highlight the moral equivalence of the two acts. Imagine that a family member would acquire great financial gain if his nephew dies. So, in the first instance, the uncle enters the bathroom where his nephew is bathing and drowns him. In the second instance, the uncle enters the bathroom intending to drown his nephew, but then the boy slips and falls into the bath. The uncle stands above the boy, ready to push his head under water if he tries to come up, but needs not do anything, and the boy dies. Rachels argues that both the action and non-action are morally equivalent, and we should thus view passive and active euthanasia as equal, morally speaking.

A principal argument against euthanasia involves the often religious-based notion of the "sanctity of life." In 1965, the Catholic Church declared it a "crime against life," though twenty-five years later they rescinded that, allowing for passive euthanasia when "inevitable death is imminent." One could justifiably consider forcing someone to die a slow, painful death against their will as *un*sanctified—even gangsters and thugs give their victims the final *coup de grâce* after they've brought them near to death (at least in the movies, anyway).

This theory that one "can't put a price on life" fails in practice. Any hospital administrator will tell you of the finite resources available; rarely, if ever, is *everything* done for *every* patient, as there simply aren't personnel and finances available for that. In some states that prohibit euthanasia, in a real linguistic sleight of hand, they have implemented the seemingly more humane "Patient Refusal of Nutrition and Hydration" (PRNH)—to avoid the immorality of actually killing a patient, they instead "allow" the already terminally ill patient to starve to death.

Where euthanasia is legal, we must be aware of the psychology of end-of-life issues. We should question to what extent someone in this fragile psychological state could truly consent to suicide free of any coercion, in much the same way a minor or intoxicated person cannot reasonably consent to various activities due to their diminished state of mind. HMOs want quicker patient turnover and stand to gain much more from the more expedient, cheaper euthanasia process. And if the patient lives in an environment that presents euthanasia as a live option, they may come to feel like a "burden" on the family and thus surrender to outside pressures. Philosopher David Velleman argues that having this option puts the burden on the patient to justify remaining alive, when (he argues) the status quo should be the opposite.

Oxymoron or not, while *good death* may not be possible, a bad death clearly is.

Oh, yes, and lest we forget the second half of the sticker . . .

YOUTH IN ASIA MADE MY TENNIS SHOES

Nike is a great case study in the power of branding. People really just want the Swoosh logo, with the shoe serving as a pedestrian billboard, much in the same way that consumers want the horse on their otherwise plain polo shirt—it sends a message to everyone that they *do* want to "Be like Mike [Jordan]," and the first step is buying his $150 shoes. With these shoes they become one step closer to being able to "Just do it," whatever "it" is. When Nike urges us to "Be like Mike," they certainly can't mean "Be born with natural athletic ability and then work really really hard to hone it." Just as the nude Abercrombie models don't actually wear the pretorn-and-wrinkled clothes they sell. But when consumers reward the advertising industry with their dollars, what else can we expect? The polo-playing symbol that signifies the fanciness of your polo shirt has quadrupled on some offerings over the past ten years. Some Tommy Hilfiger shirts devote more square inches to the logo than to the actual shirt. There is not much more room for expansion other than the symbol actually overtaking the shirt and extending outside of the actual cloth it's on, or maybe just having the shirt wearer carry around a statue of a man playing polo.

This is why Nike spent nearly $2 billion last year selling the Swoosh lifestyle through advertisements that have nothing to do with the actual product being sold. Mike could have done "it" with any ol' shoe, as evidenced by his statement "I never wore Nike shoes until I signed that Nike contract." But the extra $130 million for wearing the shoe during his career probably helped—and it helped Nike sell $130 million worth of Jordan's shoe in his first year alone.

So far so good (for Nike, anyway). But here's the catch, as illuminated by the bumper-sticker wisdom and countless books, investigative reports, and documentaries: While Nike sold $6.5 billion worth of shoes in 1996, the workers who made them earned a paltry $2.46 per day in Indonesia, and $1.60 per day in Vietnam. For a Vietnamese worker to afford the shoe he's currently working on, he would have to work for forty days without spending any of the money he's making. Worse, various news networks exposed the fact that workers in these sweatshops incur repeated physical and sexual abuse, suffering from substandard work conditions where they are forced to work sixteen-hour days. With 75 percent of Nike shoes produced in countries without independent trade unions, Nike CEO Phil Knight can continue this practice and at least maintain his current seventh-place standing in the "Richest man in the U.S." competition, coming in at a cool $5 billion by the 1990s.

Yet, capitalist extraordinaire Milton Friedman famously proposed the "one and only social responsibility of business"—to increase profits. So the argument goes. In a free market, if the job wasn't so great, sweatshop workers—including children as young as six, earning ten cents an hour—wouldn't take the job. At a Harvard University chapel, then president Lawrence Summers lectured/prayed in defense of sweatshops in his homily at morning prayers: "As long as the workers are voluntarily employed, they have chosen to work because they are working to their best alternative." But this is a bit like "choosing" to work at the factory where they only abuse you for twenty minutes instead of the usual hour at your other job. As the old sad-but-true joke goes, the only thing worse than being exploited by capitalism is not being exploited by capitalism. The lesser of two evils is still an evil.

So, yes, the bumper-sticker wisdom here really hits the mark. Though, in light of a little knowledge, we might wish for a slight tweak in Nike's logo and urge them to "Just Don't Do It."

TORTURE ONLY WORKS ON TELEVISION

Actually, torture doesn't really "work" on television any more than psychic dreams "work" in the show *Medium* or than the Brady Bunch were actually happy—it's television: It's made up. Though given that people develop such emotional ties with their television sets and the people "inside" them, one can understand that this medium might serve as the common person's psyche lab. For those doing research outside of the boob tube ("boob"—idiot), we might get a more accurate analysis. If it turns out this is wrong, we can then look at the more pressing question, "*Should* we ever torture?"

To better investigate this, we turn to those doing the fieldwork of interrogation. Army Colonel Stuart Herrington led many of the interrogations in Vietnam and claims that most common detainees provide the desired information as a result of minor "no-stress methods" of interrogation—though he also refers to the better "batting average" of more fanatical terrorists in which the success rates of "stress-free" questioning drops to about six of ten. Nothing like a little baseball talk to help illuminate torture stats. How exactly would one hit a "home run" in this scenario?

But the problem encountered with the aggressive, Jack Bauer 24-style torture is that victims will say anything to cease the pain. As Air Force Colonel John Rothrock shares, "If I take a Bunsen burner to the guy's genitals, he's going to tell you just about anything." Though it does seem that we could test the accuracy of the confessions of detainees—just go look under the rock where they said they hid the ticking time bomb. If it's not there, then turn the burner back on. It's not like we're trying to have them confess their love for us: "Tell me that you love me. And mean it."

Here the problems begin to arise for our "pro-torture" advocates, such as the potential reciprocation of other countries toward the torturing-country's soldiers, as well as creating an image of savagery and undermining an intended agenda of peace.

It's also hard to test what could have been accomplished without torture instead, as every scenario differs so greatly. "If we didn't use the Bunsen burner on you, would you have told us that anyway?" Interrogation expert Michael Koubi notes that no two people react the same way during questioning. Considered one of the most successful interrogators of our time—the proverbial Babe Ruth of the questioning world—he shares such methods as sitting quietly for hours just staring at the detainee, placing a bag over his head, or giving them a little slap or two. Certainly more humane than the human-playground-style torture at Abu Ghraib.

Of course, this forces the discussion further into defining torture. Just what qualifies as cruel and unusual? "Then I sat in a room for two hours, with the Backstreet Boys playing and no way to plug my ears." It recently surfaced that the Bush administration's all-star "torture squad"—Cheney, Rice, Rumsfeld, Powell—authorized "enhanced interrogation techniques" (EITs) but not "torture." This circumvented their definition of "torture," which includes the intent to seriously injure or kill. These EITs include waterboarding, in which a detainee is strapped down with a cloth over his face and water poured onto it, providing a "controlled drowning" scenario—the same technique employed by the likes of Pol Pot and which the United States prosecuted in war-crime trials following World War II. But they would like to make clear: It's not torture anymore, it's an EIT.

Much of the discussion of torture hinges on a utilitarian analysis: Doing these things to other humans is clearly bad/painful/unfortunate, yet the good that results—numerous innocent lives saved—clearly outweighs the harm of one terrorist in pain. In 2001, an al-Qaeda terrorist detained in Dubai was subjected to beatings and eventually divulged information that prevented an attack on a U.S. embassy. He—or more correctly, his questioners—disproved this bumper sticker in one fell swoop. Philosopher Michael Levin advocates for torture "as an acceptable measure for preventing future evils." He has us imagine that we capture a terrorist who has planted a bomb in Manhattan that will detonate that afternoon causing the death of millions. Clearly, most people would advocate any means possible in preventing this, even severe torture. Add to the scenario "a close friend or family member living in New York," and you turn the remaining naysayers into yeah-sayers.

Once one admits to this, it becomes only a matter of degree, not principle. It's reminiscent of that ol' bar ploy in which a man propositions a woman to come home with him for a million dollars. When she excitedly agrees, he renegotiates with a new offer of five dollars and she reacts out of utter disgust, "What kind of woman do you think I am!" to which he replies, "We've established that. Now we just need to agree on a price." Once you agree that torture is justified to save millions, we're only haggling over the numbers. For those with a heavy conscience, Levin provides further justification on more of a rights-based analysis, suggesting that not only did the terrorist voluntarily act in such a manner, but in doing so he "renounces civilized standards." And, if this doesn't push the conversation far enough, some prefer to introduce the "torture the terrorist's daughter" scenario, in which it seems that torturing one innocent person could potentially justify saving thousands of others.

So it turns out that torture does work, sometimes. And that there are scenarios in which most everyone justifies it, though a great many instances arise in which torture not only fails to work, but actually does more harm than good. And when you add in the inalienable rights afforded to "all members of the human family" by the United Nations (which has a much broader definition of "torture" than the torture squad's), we must reconsider our treatment of the non-fanatical detainees—maybe forcing them to watch consecutive episodes of 24 for twenty-four hours, for starters.

WE KILL PEOPLE TO SHOW PEOPLE THAT KILLING PEOPLE IS WRONG

It's hard to imagine what conceivable set of answers one must give on their career counseling test for the result to come up "Executioner." We are entertaining a pretty spooky practice: one in which medical doctors administer poison to perfectly healthy patients and sterilize the needle before doing so; where psychiatrists work tirelessly with psychologically troubled death-row patients only to then declare them fit for killing; and where doctors administer standard life-saving measures to an inmate having a heart attack only to administer life-*ending* measures the next day. With a majority of the Hollywood films that address the death penalty tilting sharply against it, we should not give them the last word (nor the first, really) and instead should examine the facts. While we oddly give celebrities clout regarding various ethical and political issues—they are celebrities, after all—we're discussing whether the government can justify killing its citizens.

In attempting to demonstrate the injustice of the death penalty, this bumper-sticker wisdom misses the mark. It's doubly wrong, as it is neither literally true nor does the not-so-subtle rhetoric constitute a consistent argument. We must first sift through the rhetoric—i.e., sarcasm—of this bumper sticker to distill the actual argument. This sticker asserts that administering the death penalty is immoral—hypocritical, even—because it kills people who break the rule "Don't kill people." It essentially disagrees with "Reciprocal Retributivism"—that we should mete out punishments most closely fitting the crime, à la "An eye for an eye."

But we can conceive of an entire fleet of bumper stickers that follow this same line of (poor) reasoning, such as the following "anti-imprisonment" parody:

WE IMPRISON PEOPLE TO SHOW PEOPLE THAT KIDNAPPING PEOPLE IS WRONG

Imagine not having a prison system, claiming that it sent the wrong message about our kidnapping taboo. Imprisonment is not kidnapping. Kidnapping involves taking someone illegally, without trial, as one might see in racy espionage films or the Bush administration's Guantánamo Bay extravaganza. Parking fines do not constitute stealing. And the death penalty is not murdering. We can't have the law set in place yet criticize it for "being above the law." Some logician at some point in ancient Greece must have stated the logical rule "A thing cannot be above itself."

Invalidating this "killing endorses killing" anti-death-penalty argument is not enough for our "pro-death" advocates to begin their guilt-free, eye-for-an-eye-gouging ways. The burden of proof is on them. And quite a burden it is, trying to find a way to justify our government killing its citizens. Our death-penalty abolitionist has the easy task of defending the correct conclusion. They just need to defend it properly.

En route to doing so, death-penalty adversaries encounter various philosophical gadflies, such as the following popular bumper-sticker wisdom:

THE DEATH PENALTY ISN'T FOR MAKING EXAMPLES, IT'S FOR MAKING BAD PEOPLE DEAD

But since 1900, the United States has executed twenty-three inno-cent people. And in the last thirty years another 130 people have been released from death row for wrongful conviction. The most common flaws found in these capital punishment trials involves false confessions, lab error, eyewitness misidentification, and jail-house informants—with massively reduced prison sentences on the line, these "snitches" will throw just about anyone under the bus, as it were. Additionally, the poor and minorities receive the death penalty in severely disproportionate numbers compared to the numbers committing capital crimes, and a murderer is consid-erably more likely to get the death penalty for killing a white man than a black man. As one of history's most oft-quoted nuns, Sister Helen Prejean writes that government "can't be trusted to control its own bureaucrats or collect taxes equitably or fill a pothole, much less decide which of its citizens to kill." So it turns out that the death penalty is also for killing some of our innocent, unjustly tried minority neighbors as well.

All that aside—after all, no system is perfect—if the govern-ment kills a few hundred citizens for the sake of some greater good or "justice," isn't that allowable? It's hard to tell just how this bumper-sticker wisdom justifies its claim of "making bad people dead" in support of the death penalty. There are basically three ways to rationalize a government punishing its citizens. And while we hold a government to a higher standard than we do parents, we can imagine the same rationale for a parent to justify punishing a child:

Utilitarianism—The punishment results in a *greater good*. Sending Johnny to his room for hitting Jimmy prevents

him from doing it again and deters others from doing it
in the future.

Retributivism—The punishment gives the malefactor what
he deserves. By hitting Jimmy, Johnny earns the bed-
room sentence as a just punishment for violating
Jimmy's rights. It's akin to when Johnny's teacher responds to his poor-grade protests, "I don't give grades,
students *earn* them."

Rehabilitivism—The punishment reforms the delinquent.
Sitting in his room for an hour "thinking about what he
did" will result in a better, non-hitting Johnny.

The reader surely sees how our bumper-sticker owner clearly
can't defend the death penalty by the last option.

It is also unlikely that the person is a utilitarian, as the first
phrase of the bumper sticker overturns a bedrock concept of that
theory: deterrence—i.e., "making examples." Having the death
penalty in place *theoretically* causes other would-be murderers
looming in our neighborhoods to refrain from murdering us. We
can imagine the death penalty given for speeding infractions and
how that might seriously deter speeding on the highways. "Deterrence" is a very popular position for death-penalty advocates.

While George Bush served as governor of Texas—the leader in
death-penalty killings among the states—he commented, "I think
the reason to support the death-penalty is because it saves other
people's lives." But instead of just "thinking" about this, if one actually looks at the facts behind it they will find it unsubstantiated.
In countries and states where capital punishment was abolished,
the murder rate did not increase as the theory of deterrence pre-
dicts. Would-be murderers just don't carry out such deliberate
thought processes as, "If I get caught, I will *only* have to sit in
prison for the remainder of my life instead of getting the death
penalty, so I'll go through with it." The threat of life imprisonment
proves equally effective in deterring people from a killing spree.

And there's the proverbial nail in the death-penalty advocate's
coffin: our inalienable right to life. The operative term being "in-

alienable"—unable to be forfeited or taken away. So even if our sticker owner is content killing innocents and unfairly favoring the deaths of certain citizens (even while spending more to do it), it turns out that they've still got some work to do with their poorly executed argument. Or they can lay it to rest, catch up with over one hundred other countries and the educated portion of the population, and buy a new sticker.

AGAINST ABORTION? THEN DON'T HAVE ONE!

Imagine a child's response to his parents scolding him for cheating on an exam: "Against cheating? Then don't cheat!" This child has clearly missed the point of morality. Actually, he—and the bumper-sticker wisdom here—is stuck in psychologist Lawrence Kohlberg's lowest level of moral development. This *pre*-conventional thinker views morality more as a guide to fulfilling one's own interests versus acting on behalf of some deeper moral principle. It *de*-scribes what they do versus *pre*scribing what we *should* do.

To further modify it, thus making it completely outlandish, imagine proclaiming, "Against murder? Then don't murder anyone!"—the exclamation point only driving home how little one may have thought this through, as we must chalk this up to the emotion-center of the brain, versus the more calculated analytical, logical locale. The murder-version is essentially how the pro-life contingent views the above bumper sticker. It has the added misfortune of providing a catalyst for antagonistic argument, spawning more name-calling and enlarged-bumper-sticker-style picketing than progressive discussion and debate.

For a majority of society, this topic presents itself as the mother of all drawing-a-line-in-the-sand exercises. On the one hand, most people do not view a collection of cells barely visible to the naked eye as a human being, much less as a person with moral rights, yet the overwhelming majority also consider abortion on the day prior to the birth of the fetus as morally abhorrent. It certainly wouldn't hold up for one to treat this particular issue like one would a matter of taste—"Don't like Vegemite? Then don't eat it!" Simply ignoring someone else performing such an act the day prior to birth would be unacceptable. The major challenge in this debate involves drawing a hard line: When, if ever, may we infringe upon the rights of a woman to her body in favor of those of the human fetus?

Philosopher Mary Anne Warren argues that once the organism becomes a moral person, then that organism has a right to life. For her, moral personhood requires much more than human DNA, as a collection of cells the day following conception is hardly a person. The criteria she provides for moral personhood include consciousness, reasoning, self-motivated activity, the capacity to communicate, and self-awareness. Many philosophers and policymakers consider this list as too narrow, as it wrongly excludes certain moral persons from the category, such as a newborn baby, and of course the sci-fi collection of characters who will soon be visiting us, such as reasoning aliens and self-aware androids.

Determining when the sperm-and-egg becomes a moral person poses a real challenge. Some other suggestions include when the fetus:

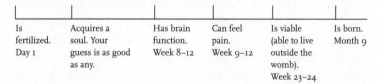

Is fertilized. Day 1	Acquires a soul. Your guess is as good as any.	Has brain function. Week 8–12	Can feel pain. Week 9–12	Is viable (able to live outside the womb). Week 23–24	Is born. Month 9

In answering the question "When does personhood begin?" bioethicist Baruch Brody has taken a "think outside of the box" approach, starting with the question "When does personhood *end?*" (or, in the commencing-of-a-new-phase approach, "When does *death* begin?"). The experts of the medical community answer: brain death. So when "McDreamy" announces "Time of death" on *Grey's Anatomy,* he correctly does so when the patient's brain has ceased working for thirty minutes—that person is no longer a person. Working backward, then, Brody suggests that when an organism with human DNA acquires this proverbial *élan vital*, it has thus *become* a person in the moral sense.

Though even if we were to agree on some essential designator such as Brody's brain function, many other relevant issues arise. Three popular concerns include the notion of "potential personhood"—that a fetus will likely develop into a full moral person, and thus we should preemptively afford that fetus said rights; the concern about abortion creating a "culture of death" as coined by Pope John Paul II, which often ties into the "sanctity of life" ethic nicely summarized by English writer Malcolm Muggeridge, "Either life is always and in all circumstances sacred, or intrinsically of no account; it is inconceivable that it should be in some cases the one, and in some the other"; and an overarching worry surrounding just what level of involvement philosophers and the government should have with the freedoms of women.

Regardless, suggesting to another that she simply refrain from doing what she views as immoral while still allowing all others to do so seems to more closely resemble the kindergarten playground than any adult forum at least minimally interested in clear thinking. The Aussies should feel free to continue eating their Vegemite sandwiches if they so choose—no judgment here (though, yuck!). But if they start lying and cheating, we should wag our finger and judge them a little.

IF WE'RE NOT SUPPOSED TO EAT ANIMALS, HOW COME THEY'RE MADE OF MEAT?

You're made of meat, are we supposed to eat you? This sounds a little bit like the same oversight made in the book of Genesis when God instructs us that "Every moving thing that is alive shall be food for you." Good thing Adam and Eve clearly weren't listening to God during that time, because if one of them took Him literally, we might not be here today. How, then, do we determine who we can eat (if anyone), on whom we can test (not just to cure disease, but to see which eyeliner melts our eyes), and who we can use solely for entertainment (bullfighting, circuses, etc.)? Princeton philosopher Peter Singer has an answer.

Singer begins his line of reasoning by revisiting the (now) obviously immoral examples of sexism and racism. Both the sexist and racist discriminate based on irrelevant factors. Granted, one can find myriad differences among the sexes—so much so that a book about them being from different planets becomes a bestseller—but no single difference allots rights to one group (say, the right to vote, or to life) over another. Likewise with race—during the time of slavery, even though "Everyone was doing it," and slaves were "just three-fifths of a person," no *rational* justification existed. Likewise, Singer argues, with species. While many differences exist, there are none so morally relevant as to give unequal moral consideration among species. To do so would make one a *speciesist* (he apologizes for the term though it has now become the bedrock for animal rights).

Philosopher Paul Copan nicely frames a common counter to Singer's clever position. He undercuts the entire system of secular ethics in asking "Why think that *anything* has value if all organisms have emerged from valueless processes?" He provides an answer to his own rhetoric: We can't, so morality must come from the gods. But to start, we *do* have rights, and they do mean something. In the same way we have numbers. If one erases the number three, they haven't destroyed the number three. We don't say that because God didn't assign value to the number three that it's therefore completely empty. Even more so on behalf of morality, we don't have a "numerical conscience" in the way our moral conscience perks up when we see harm done to an animal. So here's the deal: You agree to get rid of numbers and then we'll see about eradicating morality.

Copan goes on to run a page-long list of qualities that humans have that animals do not, thus affording the former a morally significant life. He includes such things as self-awareness, an ability to "rise above . . . and reflect on" the environment, an understanding of death, ability to create culture, ability to meaningfully express relationships through language, and countless others. But as Singer points out, no human infant, nor severely retarded or senile person, can do any of these things either. Additionally, some animals are even better at some of these pursuits than those humans, such as chimpanzees who can recognize themselves in the mirror (or at least use it to clean their teeth, which is more than we can say for most infants). As Singer writes, to mark the boundary of moral consideration by a "characteristic like intelligence or rationality would be to mark it in an arbitrary manner. Why not choose some other characteristic, like skin color?"

To turn to the world's various religions for guidance provides no help, as they all offer somewhat contradictory (and often quite odd) regulations. Hinduism holds cows as sacred and not to be touched, which often creates quite a spectacle as locals stop to permit them to roam through traffic. Judaism prohibits adherents from eating "unclean," non-kosher meats (animals that chew their cud and have cloven hooves), thus ruling out a majority of animals for dinner such as shellfish, escargots, vultures, bats, and Tasmanian devils. And from the Bible we learn that even your ox must rest on the Sabbath (along with your ass and manservants), and that an abundantly sinful town can put their sins in/on a goat and send it out to the wilderness to be eaten, thus eating the sins with it. If someone gets your goat, as they say, may they not get your *scape*-goat and all of your bad deeds with it.

Finally, just before Copan concludes that we must "deny that animals have rights," he suggests that we can still gain much from them, such as the entertainment they provide. He reminisces about the "dancing bears that had been trained to do remarkable (and hilarious) feats." Sounds like an awful time for bears—being caged, whipped, "taught" how to stand on one foot, and have a ball bounced off their faces. This so-called benefit of animals compares with how enjoyable it is for biblical-style manservants to "dance" while we shoot bullets at their feet. Good bear. Good slave. Carl Cohen provides a more logically valid argument, much along the lines of the numbers-and-morality discussion. Because morality is a human construct, he argues, it thus applies only to humans. This explains why we don't judge a lion for killing and eating a baby zebra but we certainly would if a human acted likewise to another human. Since animals don't play the Morality Game, they aren't restricted by its rules, nor, as is the case here, do they benefit from them.

Singer argues that one quality does exist that should drive our assigning moral consideration to the sexes, races, and species: the capacity to suffer. This moral fact drives our intuition as to why it is allowable to kick a rock down the street but wrong to do so to a mouse, why it is wrong for the precocious schoolboy to slowly burn the legs off an ant with his magnifying glass, and why it is wrong (or should be) to permit such institutions as bullfighting—in which they first torture a bull, then run it to exhaustion, have a man on a horse stab it with a sword in the neck, followed by others prodding it so it bleeds profusely, then have the "brave" matador kill the bull hours later in its delirious state.

In a final attempt to demonstrate our rights over animals, we hear that we are made in the image of God. Though as other bumper-sticker wisdom sarcastically prods,

IF HUMANS ARE MADE IN GOD'S IMAGE THEN WHY AREN'T WE INVISIBLE TOO?

Until we solve these puzzles and overcome Singer's challenge—because who wants to be a speciesist?—at the least, cosmetic animal testing, torture, and "entertainment" can be put on hold for a bit and we can keep in mind that we're all made of meat.

LANGUAGE
A Sticker's Worth 1,000 Words

IF A MAN SPEAKS IN THE FOREST AND THERE'S NO WOMAN THERE TO HEAR HIM, IS HE STILL WRONG?

Not necessarily. But he may not be right either. And while we're plodding along through stereotypes, he probably ended up there because he was lost and unwilling to ask for directions, likely too busy listening to the baseball game to even care.

As for the deeper insight behind the nature of this question . . . Ludwig Wittgenstein posited that any sort of private language would render the so-called language meaningless. The internally secretive speaker would have no standard by which to judge the correctness of an utterance. Imagine growing up on a deserted island and pondering, "*Inaspofi sl sl Zepong?*" How would you even think to ask such a question? How would you know if you correctly answered it? But when a shipwreck victim lands on the island, you can point to *this* and say, "*Zepong.*" And when you point to *that* instead, calling it a "*Zepong,*" your newfound friend corrects you, pointing to *this,* uttering, "*Zepong.*" This all assumes you each know how to follow the convention of "index finger pointing," still unknown to dogs and not universal among humans. Rule following, like language use, requires a community to establish it—a dog doesn't follow the rule "Bark when you hear a knock." So, as Wittgenstein clearly concludes, "The meaning of a word is its use in the language." The public discourse of checks and balances is the magic needed to give meaning to otherwise meaningless utterances—our man wouldn't even have to be alone in the forest for this to be the case. Empathy and context matter.

So, in an obvious sense, it depends what our man in the forest says. If musing "Two plus two equals four," then he's not wrong, as per the agreed-upon community of language users from which he hails. If in the forest saying, *"Usaf, pao poiu,"* then he's also not wrong, but he's not right. And if he's wrong by the sexist caveat "women always find wrong in men," then he may have just been wrong in his selection of a mate.

Wittgenstein has us imagine that everyone in our current community owns a little box. In that box is something known only to the respective individual—their own Zepong. Since you can't ever see inside another's box, and no one sees inside yours, you could all have something different, or the same, or ever-changing, or nothing at all. So while we can all refer publicly to our Zepong as "the contents of the box," "Zepong" cannot refer to any one *thing* and thus has no real meaning. Wittgenstein applies this to sensations as well. When one says, "This is the *same* sensation I had yesterday," there is simply no criterion for correctness. As a private definition, it is meaningless. Plus, how could one possibly remember if it was, in fact, exactly the same? People have trouble accurately remembering physical things they saw, heard, and touched just that morning. This discussion provides an additional benefit for Wittgenstein in the battleground of ideas as it supports his conclusion that we can derive meaning through behavior. We know that someone feels the same pain as he did before through a public manifestation of the sensation in question: "Look, he's behaving the same way he did last time he touched the fire."

When our subject finally makes his way out of the forest to arrive home and, being the thoughtful guy that he is, says, "Honey, I was wrong back there in the forest," she can reply, "I highly doubt it."

ALONE IN THE FOREST REVISITED—THIS TIME WITH NO MEN

Given the historical context of this bumper sticker, it is worth revisiting to briefly shed light on the age-old question, "If a tree falls in the forest and there's no one there to hear it, does it make a sound?" The answer, per Wittgenstein, depends on what you mean by "sound." If by "sound" one means "Something that causes vibrations in the air," then yes, the tree does just that. In much the same way that one literally feels air displaced by a jet engine or a booming speaker in a nightclub, the tree too causes particle vibration— assuming it didn't fall in a vacuum. But if by "sound" one means the more common "Vibrations translated by the inner ear," then *no:* With no one there, there are no ears and thus no sound.

These insights shed light on the ideas of three other well-known philosophers. First, and possibly most extreme, George Berkeley, who went so far as to say that even *physical objects* cease to exist if no one perceives them, as summarized by his famous dictum "To be is to be perceived." So, not only does the lonely tree fail to make a noise, it fails to exist altogether, if not under the watchful eye of an omniscient Being (full disclosure: Berkeley was a bishop). John Locke, in more widely accepted fashion, distinguished between two types of qualities of an object: those inherent to the object, such as solidity and shape, and those of the senses, such as the color of an object or the sound it makes. These later qualities are not actual qualities *of* the object, but instead reside in the perceiver: How one views something is not a quality of that thing but of the viewer. If Jill thinks an apple sweet, and Jack finds it sour, these are not qualities of the apple—while we may say "The apple is sour," as if it is somehow *of* the apple, Locke shows that this is instead something in us. So sound is not *in* the tree, the ground, or the air, but *in* us. To take this to its logical conclusion, German philosopher Immanuel Kant argued that we cannot truly *know*, in the deepest sense, any object in and of itself but only objects as we observe them.

Wittgenstein warned that we are often "bewitched" by language, and this case serves as a great example. To think that falling trees *have* sound in or near them is bewitchment enough. And, thanks to Wittgenstein, we now have even greater motivation for public discourse, for deciphering right and wrong, and for really making some noise.

HUMPTY DUMPTY WAS PUSHED

The motivation to choose *this* as one's battle we'll leave to the psychologists to decipher. Though on the heels of that, it's also worth investigating whether Jack was pushed, and not by Jill. With Jack's having a crown, some Shakespearean villain could have shoved them *both* out of jealousy, for why would Jill come tumbling after, just because Jack did? Though admittedly "Jack Was Pushed" doesn't make for as catchy of a bumper sticker.

Theories on the deeper meaning in "Humpty Dumpty" fall into quite a range, from that of Humpty representing the hunchbacked King Richard III's fall from his horse in battle, to a poorly designed British tower that crumbled to disrepair, to a description of what happens if you drink too much of a boiled brandy and ale drink called "The Humpty Dumpty." This bumper-sticker wisdom touches on the "anything goes" analysis of novels, stories, and poems that turn many a high school student off from reading them in the first place: "Wait, what? When the character wearing a red sweater eats an apple she's angry about knowledge, only later to eat an orange while wearing blue to show her sadness at the loss of youth?"

Referred to as postmodernism, this is more of a non-theory theory. It assumes that no objective reality exists and so we can only *create* truth, not discover it. It fails to account for all of those pesky authors sharing their ideas and discoveries of human nature, and those scientists who think they are actually curing diseases, building airplanes, and discovering fossils.

In *Through the Looking Glass,* mathematician and logician Lewis Carroll utilizes Humpty in what can only be classified as Science Fiction's distant cousin, Logic Fiction:

> "When I use a word," Humpty Dumpty said in a rather scornful tone, "it means just what I choose it to mean—neither more nor less."

"The question is," said Alice, "whether you can make words mean different things."

"The question is," said Humpty Dumpty, "which is to be master—that's all."

Clearly, we cannot use words to mean whatever we want, for in that case, they become meaningless. When Humpty haphazardly uses "glory" to mean "a nice knock-down argument," we realize that something has gone awry. Some theologians employ a similar linguistic sleight of hand in their attempt to justify evils such as the Holocaust and deadly tsunamis in light of an all-loving, all-powerful God, suggesting that this is part of a loving God's plan. But if their definition of "love" can include the murder of 5.8 million innocent people, then we might as well be speaking to Father Dumpty.

The Taoist approach to language in a sense embraces this very problem of language, though maybe overreacts a bit. It is best summarized by the proverb "The instant you speak about a thing you miss the mark." Because language is so inexact and imprecise, in merely attempting to describe something like the "true nature and overarching oneness of the universe," one inevitably fails. It creates quite the conundrum for someone hoping to learn about Taoism as, by definition, anyone who talks about it does not know. And the hiring process of universities in search of an expert in Eastern Mysticism poses a unique challenge as well, for as Lao Tzu reminds us, "He who knows does not speak."

As a possible response to Humpty's question of which is to be master, you or the words, Richard Dawkins suggests, "Words are our servants, not our masters." This might be a more reasonable attempt to find middle ground between the mute Taoist and the freewheeling postmodern Humpty.

Humpty Dumpty clearly did not die in vain. At the least, he is a martyr for all the authors, poets, and artists who actually do mean something when they write.

. . . .

The HELP STAMP OUT BUMPER STICKERS *Segment*

. . . .

THIS IS NOT A BUMPER STICKER

Well . . . yes it is. With that out of the way we can get down to the crux of things.

We turn again to Ludwig Wittgenstein for insight as he addressed this general issue in his use of the notion of a language game. He argued that words acquire meaning through their *use* by a community as opposed to their all sharing some common element. Try this simple exercise with friends. List the features common to all games that distinguish "game" from *all other* activities. This often proves to be futile as we end up excluding things considered games or including any activity such as test-taking, driving, and things as broad as the "game" of life. Thus, Wittgenstein seems vindicated as he imagined this pursuit to be similar to the fly trapped in a bottle that repeatedly flies into the sides of the glass in hopes of gaining freedom.

In an attempt to "show the fly the way out of the bottle," have that same group determine which of the following constitutes a game: bullfighting, Olympic ballroom dancing, Russian roulette, boxing, Frisbee, war. Most groups split right down the middle, thus discrediting Wittgenstein somewhat. If words acquire meaning through agreement from a community of language-users, then a small community should be able to agree on something as simple as "game."

Wittgenstein quips in his *Philosophical Investigations*, "Philosophy is a struggle against the bewitchment of our understanding by means of language." So maybe it's as easy as this simple rule: If it acts like a bumper sticker, and sticks like a bumper sticker, and looks like a bumper sticker, then it's probably a bumper sticker. The question is, if you place a bumper sticker on a wall, does it morph into a Wall Sticker?

ALL EXTREMISTS SHOULD BE SHOT

That's a little extreme, don't you think? (Couldn't resist.) Hopefully for this person's sake they drive in a favorable "Guns Don't Kill People . . ." bumper-sticker environment. But they're just making a point, and a bumper sticker that reads "Don't Be So Extreme," or "Extreme: Bad. Run of the Mill: Good" wouldn't drive home the point as well; it wouldn't be extreme enough to get our fleeting attention.

ALL GENERALIZATIONS ARE FALSE, INCLUDING THIS ONE

True, kind of. But as soon as it's true, it's false. It's similar to the historical paradox "This sentence is false." If that's true, then it's false. And if false, then it's true.

The bumper-sticker wisdom is certainly false in the sense that generalizations themselves are not completely true. For example, although we say men are stronger than women, some women are physically stronger than some men. Thus, they are merely generalizations, approximations. No generalization is exactly true (yes, including this one). That's the problem with speaking *generally.* But they are true *in general,* which can be useful, generally speaking.

All semantics aside, this is an insight into the self-defeating nature of that pesky theory of relativism, which states: All truths are relative, thus no statement is absolutely true. It turns out that this disproves itself right from the get-go. Since it is a statement, then it cannot be absolutely true by its own proclamation. Plus, it would result in no one ever being wrong about anything, which, among other problems, would eradicate the need for the entire profession of teaching.

MODERATION ONLY IN MODERATION

That is, sometimes you should go overboard and be excessive, totally fly off the handle and let loose, live in the world of extremes. But only in moderation, of course. Sometimes you should do nothing too. Absolutely nothing. Aristotle wrote, "It is better to rise from life as from a banquet—neither thirsty nor drunken." In doing so, he framed his guide to the good life, the Doctrine of the Mean: In our lives, we should strive to find the mean between two extremes, in this case, neither imbibing so much we're stumbling home, nor so little that we can't take the edge off, enjoy, or at least quench our thirst.

ALWAYS REMEMBER YOU'RE UNIQUE, JUST LIKE EVERYONE ELSE

"Hey, wait a minute. If I am just like everyone else then that's the antithesis of unique. Being like everyone else makes me ordinary. Nice try, buttering me up and telling me I'm special and extraordinary. *Extra* ordinary, yes. More like *super* ordinary. The *most* ordinary person ever. Now that would be unique."

SOME QUESTIONS HAVE NO ANSWERS

Like what?

ON THE ADVICE OF LEGAL COUNSEL, THIS BUMPER STICKER CONTAINS NO MESSAGE

The bumper-sticker version of pleading the Fifth—though a blank bumper sticker might have gotten the message across a bit more concisely, albeit more obscurely. This message somewhat resembles the "No comment" often given in response to a potentially accusatory question that itself *is* a sort of comment—if you didn't steal the money, why not reply "No" instead of "No comment"?

And in light of these self-defeating bumper stickers, why no one has ever printed up George Bernard Shaw's "Never take anybody's advice" advice, we'll never know. They should.

And where is "Ignore This Bumper Sticker"?

. . . .

WHAT HAPPENS IF A HORSE AND CART RUNS OVER A CHICKEN AND EGG?

I was chomping at the bit, so to speak, to answer this bass-ackward bit of rhetoric, primarily because it would allow me to get up on my high horse and solve that infamous chicken-and-egg question that is so strangely pesky. I'm actually surprised so many people have cared for so long, though I am still more surprised that we're seeking answers to why one of the aforementioned perpetrators crossed the road.

To put the cart before the horse and first divulge the solution, the *chicken* came first. It's actually quite a simple solution, though it assumes that you accept the facts of evolution. If not, then you can consult your favorite creation myth—such as Genesis, in which the answer is still "chicken," though this answer is supported by God simply saying "Let the birds fly" on the fourth day of creation, and not "Let there be eggs." The answers from all the myths throughout history vary so much that you may find that you prefer to put your eggs in this basket—*all* of them. Plus, what kind of all-powerful supernatural being would sit on an egg when He can get the chicken for free?

Back to actual facts. By definition, a member of a species can lay an egg only of that species. This bit of insight illuminates the obtuse quote of Confucius, "The daughter of a crab does not give birth to a bird." (Talk about getting it straight from the horse's mouth.) Given this, then, non-chickens laid non-chicken eggs for a long while. Then, that one golden egg had a mutation that led to the first chicken. And that chicken then laid the first chicken-egg. Chicken first. Chicken egg second.

You can likely see the involvement (and inherent problem of) definitions in this solution that permeate many of our major metaphysical problems, though delving into this is a horse of another color. Nevertheless it resonates with Aristotle's logic as he purportedly wrote, "There could not have been a first egg to give a beginning to birds, or there would have been a first bird which gave a beginning to eggs; for a bird comes from an egg."

Given the historical roots of the chicken-and-egg question, it clearly came before the saying "Putting the cart before the horse," which first appeared in print in Robert Whittington's *Vulgaria* in 1527. And this one is easier—the horse comes first, or at least it should, though distilling the deeper virtue of the bumper-sticker wisdom in this case requires putting the cart before the horse, as we are assuming the chicken crossed the road in the first place.

POLITICS AND SOCIETY
You're Right to Pursue Happiness

VISUALIZE WORLD PEACE

It's hard to go wrong here. This bumper-sticker wisdom doesn't demand that we really *do* anything. Just visualize. Daydream about it. And aside from a few outlying vigilantes, who wouldn't want this? In John Lennon's words, "Imagine all the people / Living life in peace." The hope is that this vision so captivates us that it actually motivates us to act: "And the world will live as one." Though he also asks us to imagine no religion (and thus, no heaven), no countries, and "Nothing to kill or die for." And herein lies the catch. We make the move from romantic idealism—how we wish things were—to realism—how things really are.

Ideally, we participate in Nature as what Jean-Jacques Rousseau famously called Noble Savages. Noble—kind and good; Savages—people, namely Indians, living without formal government. The idea is that before humans are thrust into the constructs of "society," they live peacefully and in noble fashion. As Rousseau wrote, "Everything is good leaving in the hands of the Creator of Things; everything degenerates in the hands of man."

After we finish straining to pat ourselves (and our ancestors) on our collective backs for being so darned good, many anthropologists demonstrate this to be simply false (warning: realism ahead). Harvard psychologist Steven Pinker points out that we have actually become *more* noble and *less* violent with the development of formal societies. Evidence shows that life in *pre*-civilized societies exhibited considerably higher rates of extreme violence and lack of concern for human life. The numbers killed in all of the wars of the twentieth century would have to result in 2 billion deaths—instead of the (mere) 100 million—in order to consistently match the death tolls of tribal societies. Additionally, he reminds us that we rarely if ever carry out various *ignoble* practices common until relatively recent history, such as "Cruelty as entertainment, human sacrifice to indulge superstition, . . . torture and mutilation as routine punishment," and many others.

So if we're not naturally good, then our standard black-and-white calculus deduces that we must be bad, or even evil. One problem standing in our way of this goodness is greed—what the Roman poet Ovid termed the "cursed love of having," which inevitably results in conflict and even war. The Darth Vader of the debate, seventeenth-century philosopher Thomas Hobbes, plays the role of defense counsel against the Skywalkerian Rousseau. Most famously he suggested that without any formal society and with everyone having a right to everything else, inevitably two people will want the same thing, which unavoidably leads to conflict. So in our natural state, life would be "solitary, poor, nasty, brutish, and short." Basically, two guys want the same thing, and with no law dissuading them, the one has a quick "war" against the other. Ad infinitum.

While that may be depressing, the glimmer of hope is that with this realism we create a worldview—a view of ourselves—that is honest. A collective, looking our 6.8 billion selves in the mirror. From this vantage point, we can truly make informed decisions as we continue to coexist.

All of this might explain the parody of a response to our romantic bumper-sticker wisdom:

VISUALIZE WHIRLED PEAS

While also difficult, at least it's not something that flies in the face of human nature and is also something beneficial for our human bodies. Plus, it can be fun to imagine "People living life in peas."

WORK HARDER: MILLIONS ON WELFARE DEPEND ON YOU

Since a majority of bumper stickers don't make it onto cars valued at over $40,000, it's hard to imagine who's flaunting this bumper-sticker wisdom. High-end cars have forgone the use of bumper-car-style bumpers anyway, instead extending the shiny car frame down a bit. It's as if having a bumper concedes that one will be bumping into things—"Not me. I *earned* this car. I won't be bumping into stuff with it."

To shed some light on this bumper-sticker wisdom, imagine what a village of potential car owners would look like if we extrapolated the United States population down to 100 people. This village that you inhabit has 14 illiterate members and 27 who have a college education; 5 of the villagers earn a third of the village's entire income, while 6 of them earn less than .3 percent of it; 40 of them think and hope your village is headed toward a biblical end-times Armageddon; and 7 of them own a Britney Spears album.

With this economic disparity of your village, you have two very general options. The one, clearly opposed by this bumper-sticker owner, is that the most well-to-do help out the least well off. Aptly termed "distributive justice," this is sort of the Robin Hood approach of "Steal from the rich to give to the poor." But it's not stealing if it's justified, right? So says the most famous of champions for this view, philosopher John Rawls. He has us imagine viewing our village wearing theoretical blinders—a "Veil of Ignorance"—that prevent us from seeing our own status in the village regarding our wealth and natural abilities. From this standpoint of fairness, he suggests we would rationally do whatever benefits the least well off—it's sort of like when your mom lets you cut the cake with you choosing the last piece so you cut them all equally. In this case, if you were to come into this village inheriting the wealth of your parents, you won't be that much the worse for losing a chunk of that money, compared to the great gain if you are on the other end of the born-into-riches lottery receiving a Robin Hood–style handout.

And in the right corner, also hailing from Harvard University: philosopher Robert Nozick. Contrary to Rawls, Nozick's "libertarianism" more closely reflects that famous French term *laissez-faire,* literally to "let things alone." In this case, with everyone in your village truly free, they are also free to exchange goods and services as they see fit, without the government "stealing" some of their time and money to give to others. Nozick equates heavy taxation with "forced labour," as some villagers must work in order to give to others—sort of a reversed slavery as though the poor downtrodden villagers are sitting around sipping lemonade while the five rich villagers fly around in their jets, sending a check every week.

It all comes down to a question of "What is fair?" Imagine that two of our villagers board an airplane together, one six foot six and the other five foot one. As they sit down, the taller one says, "This isn't fair. We both paid the same but you have much more leg room." The shorter passenger shrugs his shoulders, asking, "Should we cut your legs off to spite your body?" "That doesn't make any sense." "My point exactly." In some situations, it *is* feasible to adjust the proverbial airplane seats a bit to provide similar leg room for all—even those born into a situation completely out of their control—so that they may at least enjoy the basic liberties of life without infringing too much on those born into the luxurious first-class.

FREE TIBET

An advertising campaign put to good use. If you spend any time on the roads, you've seen this bumper-sticker command but likely don't know what you're supposed to do. "Me? Should I free Tibet?" Most people don't know why Tibet is even "un-free" or where it is in the first place. This can be deduced from the 2006 Roper Poll in which 60 percent of Americans were unable to locate Iraq on a map, despite the country's recent "Mission Accomplished"—though to avoid a critique of ethnocentrism, half of the subjects couldn't find Mississippi either.

When China became Communist in 1949, it claimed the adjacent Tibet by force as Chinese territory. Five years later the not-so-aptly named Chinese People's Liberation Army had taken over. They repeatedly bombed and pillaged the country and publicly tortured and wrongfully arrested the noble members, monks, and citizens in the predominantly Buddhist country. Their needless violence forced thousands of Tibetans to flee their homes, along with Tibet's spiritual leader, the Dalai Lama. Today, the Chinese continue to rule the country, keeping thousands of Tibetans imprisoned for so-called political dissent, where they consistently suffer inhumane treatment. The Dalai Lama has worked diligently to establish peace, earning the Nobel Peace Prize in 1989, while still bound by the Buddhist ethic of non-violence (*ahimsa*). Accurate reporting about Tibet is slow to spread as the Chinese monitor the information in and out to the tune of regulating Internet searches and threatening with imprisonment and torture anyone who dissents (thus, a ghostwriter penned this entry).

The clear-cut concern hinges on the purely philosophical concept of *rights*. We all hear the term repeatedly without thinking much of it. The American reader has a right not only to life, but also to liberty and to the additional right to try to get happy, as denoted in the "guide book," The Declaration of Independence. For those not fortunate enough to live under that umbrella, the United Nations has a list of thirty rights afforded to all citizens of the world (thus making Americans doubly endowed). It is these U.N. rights upon which China infringes; as one Free-Tibet website indicts, "So fundamental is the denial of basic human rights in Tibet that it would be more appropriate to talk about human wrongs." So where are these rights? Who gives them to us and by what authority? What color are they? Can we return them for cash or credit?

"Right" is an admittedly abstract idea, one of those things that most everyone knows from far away, but which up close can blind us. One source of rights, suggested by John Locke and Immanuel Kant, is nature: We have *natural rights* such as the right to "life, liberty, and property." Natural rights, then, exist regardless of any government and are literally part of the natural order of things. Kant based this discovery on reason. Locke, on the other hand, derived them from God. The Declaration of Independence shows Locke's influence in the famous words "We hold these truths to be self-evident, that all men are created equal, that they are endowed by their Creator with certain unalienable Rights." Unfortunately, for some, this is not so "self-evident"—either that, or they throw up their arms and say, "Infringement upon rights? Yeah, so what?"

The founder of utilitarianism, Jeremy Bentham, refers to natural rights as not just "nonsense" but "Nonsense upon stilts." Instead of some nebulous idea of metaphysical rights, he argued we do clearly have *legal* rights—those granted to us by the mere fact that we live in a governed society. This derives from his moral theory of utilitarianism, which fits nicely into one catch phrase: "The greatest happiness for the greatest number." No natural rights, just making as many people happy for as much of the time as possible. Sort of a McDonald's "We love to see you smile" theory (minus the frowning when you later become obese).

Regardless of one's stance on the ontology of rights, something has clearly gone awry in Tibet. It's hard to disagree with the Dalai Lama in his 1993 address to the U.N.:

> The key to creating a better and more peaceful world is the development of love and compassion for others . . . It is not enough to merely state that all human beings must enjoy equal dignity. This must be translated into action.

Love, compassion, equal dignity, and action based on these virtues. Dare we say this might be something we can all agree on?

THE MOST VIOLENT ELEMENT IN SOCIETY IS IGNORANCE

I'm not sure who said it best or if these two people have ever been referenced in the same sentence: Hitler or Plato. From Hitler comes the rather frightening "Thank goodness for those in power that people don't know how to think." Plato anticipated this (somewhat) in his Allegory of the Ship. The captain of a ship, like the ruler of a country, must be astute in a myriad of fields, from law to physics, to astronomy and economics, to geography and engineering. To have the shipmates and passengers and all those aboard weigh in on each of the captain's decisions would cause mayhem and, in Plato's allegory, lead to eventual mutiny. So Plato conveniently held that the Philosopher Kings should instead rule the republic in a sort of monarchy, as they have access to the essence of all that is good.

America, though, is a democracy. And ignorance displayed by the people casting votes and by the elected "captains" can be quite dangerous—can even lead to violence—as they collectively decide on issues entrenched in various topics such as economics (e.g., taxes), biology (stem cell research, global warming), history (foreign policy), sociology, psychology, astronomy, law, and many others. With decisions to steer the ship made out of ignorance, it will run aground—I leave it to the reader to choose his or her favorite end-times story to fill in how that would work within Plato's analogy.

Unfortunately, the shipmates of America's current ship seem unqualified to advise captains, as they exhibit very little knowledge of the ship to begin with, as evidenced by these low-lights:

In 1996, only 33 percent could name their congressman, 6 percent knew who served as the Chief Justice, and about one in five knew there are one hundred senators and that senators serve six-year terms. Only 54 percent of high school graduates knew which party controlled the House of Representatives (versus 77 percent in 1947). And in 2000, only 6 percent could name the Speaker of the House compared to 66 percent who could name the host of the television show *Who Wants to Be a Millionaire*. Then again, a 2004 national poll showed that the public supported a constitutional amendment that allowed marriage only between a man and a woman. Yet in the same poll they also agreed that "Defining marriage was not an important enough issue to be worth changing the Constitution." Clearly, American voters want the impossible: to amend the Constitution while not amending it. Maybe this says more about polls and the voter than it does about views of marriage, as another poll given by more crafty pollsters showed that 40 percent of Americans have an opinion regarding the Public Affairs Act of 1975—an act that doesn't even exist.

As for knowledge of the universe, we didn't do much better. One adult in five thinks the sun revolves around the earth and only 49 percent know that it takes a year for the earth to orbit the sun. Only 22 percent could properly define a molecule and just 48 percent know that electrons are smaller than atoms. Even before the 2004 election, when the stem cell issue occupied the forefront of politics, over a third of adults surveyed had never heard of a stem cell. And only 48 percent of Americans know that the earliest humans did not live at the same time as the dinosaurs, while 55 percent do not know what DNA—the basic unit of heredity—is.

While knowing how electrons interact with the rest of the molecule may not be relevant in our daily lives, at least a terse understanding of what science is, how it works, and what knowledge it has produced can help society make informed choices. For one, it would immediately squelch popular chain emails including such non sequiturs as "If evolution is true, then why aren't there half-monkeys and half-humans walking around?" Frighteningly, for many, this bit of rhetoric serves as evidence against what many incorrectly believe to be the scientific theory of evolution.

But ignorance also results in our directly harming ourselves as well. This ignorance provides a platform on which the public comes to entrust celebrities and other "laypersons" in areas of science and medicine. The pseudo-scientific magic potion for the common cold, Airborne, so popular during the early 2000s, went through no clinical scientific trials. Actually, these fizzy pills could make a cold worse, as they include nearly 1,000 percent of one's daily vitamin C allowance along with excessive amounts of many other elements—so while your body is already fighting a cold, it has to work overtime to get rid of all the excess. And our bodies cure colds on their own. Yet people rely on anecdotal evidence as proof: "I took Airborne and then didn't get sick, therefore Airborne works!" They employ the equally vacuous "I took Airborne and my cold went away, so Airborne works!" Most days you aren't sick anyway, and when you do get sick, the average cold lasts just six to seven days. So Airborne consumption may *feel* like it works, but the $23 million class-action lawsuit that Airborne eventually lost argues otherwise.

Jenny McCarthy has also made waves in the field of science. Best known as a nude model for *Playboy* and booger-flicking host of MTV's *Singled Out*, she moved on to tackle the autism-and-vaccines controversy. She instructs the public that childhood vaccines such as Measles/Mumps/Rubella directly link to increases in autism. Not only has this been disproven in numerous scientific and legal tests, but the compound she and others blame was removed from the vaccines in 1999, yet no decrease in autism resulted. Instead, we can only assume that her dissuasion of the use of these vaccines has caused thousands of easily preventable illnesses and even numerous preventable deaths. *Playboy* models can certainly know science—just as some scientists could surely succeed in the porn industry—it's just unfortunate that they garner more attention from the public on such matters than those legitimately qualified to report it.

The religion/cult of Scientology also chimes in on the autism debate, deeming it—along with *all* mental illnesses—a fiction. That is, for all those suffering from depression, autism, schizophrenia, etc., it apparently is just all in their heads, figuratively speaking. According to doctrine, in an intergalactic genocide 75 million years ago, evil aliens used psychiatry as a tool of oppression that still goes on today. The wicked overlords transported bil-

lions of other aliens to earth in a jet and exterminated them in vol-
canoes, but their remaining tainted souls—because it's unreason-
able to expect the immaterial souls to blow up—came to inherit
our bodies today, causing all current human psychological angst.
We just need to pay Scientologists to remove them. Unfortunately,
(a) people believe this and (b) this has led to numerous preventable
deaths and suicides of its followers, though not for Scientology's
inventor, L. Ron Hubbard, who requested psychiatric treatment
near the end of his own life. Thousands of examples of harmful
pseudo-scientific and supernatural beliefs of all sorts abound even
in our modern age of scientific enlightenment. But if one is ignorant of science, then why not listen to the cutest informant or
charismatic cult leaders.

In a democracy, the shipmates do choose who drives the
ship—but as Thomas Jefferson warned, "If a nation expects to be
ignorant and free, in a state of civilization, it expects what never
was and never will be." And directly weighing in on the topic, Martin Luther King, Jr., asserts, "Nothing in all the world is more dangerous than sincere ignorance and conscientious stupidity." *Most*
violent element? It's certainly in the running.

DISSENT IS PATRIOTIC

Well, maybe not as patriotic as fighting for your country or
working as a public servant—though how could dissent be any
more patriotic than consent, or even compliance? What about that
"Coexist" bumper sticker—can't we all just get along? It turns out
that sometimes we can, almost too much so.

World-renowned psychologist Solomon Asch ran a study examining social pressures on individuals. He placed groups of six
other experimenters (his buddies) in a room and he added one
true subject—someone not in on the study. He asked him to decipher which of three lines most closely matched another line, and

one line clearly did. Each of Asch's buddies answered first, intentionally choosing incorrectly. This was enough to cause a third of the subjects to conform, choosing the obviously incorrect answer as well.

"Okay, we know, we know. Humans are sheep. Lemmings even. We can't think for ourselves. Social pressure even changes the way we *see* things, or causes us to report false conclusions rather than be seen as a (gulp) *dissenter*." But that's not the only point relevant here (though interesting analysis).

Asch then conducted the same experiment with one small change. He added a single buddy to disagree with the others before our true subject had a chance to answer. And even if the dissenter disagreed in the *wrong* way—choosing line A when the group chose B but the answer was clearly C—this nearly quadrupled the chances that the subject would voice his true opinion. It turns out that we just need some other sap to be wrong, so we can more freely be wrong ourselves. Or in this case, right.

Now add this to nineteenth-century British philosopher John Stuart Mill's defense of free speech, and you get one step closer to a better democracy. Mill claimed that in squelching the true sharing of opinion, we deprive the human race of potential truths and also rob the dissenter even more. For if we silence a potential opinion, then either that opinion was right—in which case we miss out on exchanging truth for error—or the opinion was wrong, and we not only miss out on countless opportunities to say "I told you so," but we lose the "livelier impression of truth, produced by its collision with error." It's as though we would become even *more* right than we were before hearing a wrongheaded idea, because now our correct opinion has survived yet another contest on the intellectual battlefield. Fourth-century philosopher Epicurus reminds arguers that "In a philosophical dispute, he gains most who is defeated, since he learns the most." See, being wrong can be a good thing. Then again, Mill also said that it's better to be a dissatisfied Socrates than a satisfied pig, so he does seem maybe a little too keen on dissension.

All of this doesn't mean we should get unlimited free speech.

It all comes back to one famous simple analogy that, as usual, doesn't provide that precision we want: You can't yell "Fire!" in a crowded theater without the perceived threat of fire. Even though you do have free speech—and sometimes you just want to *speak* "Fire" to everyone at a movie—it can't infringe on other more important rights such as a right to life and to not being harmed. This analogy has been applied to everything from the harm done by pornography to the harm done by handing out antiwar pamphlets urging dissenters to head to Canada where the hockey is better. Lawyers even applied it to the harm done by a woman on a Southwest flight wearing a T-shirt referring to the Bush administration with an expletive; she was asked to leave because of it. It turns out the test for discerning "harm" is a lot like that used in the Supreme Court for pornography—"I'll know it when I see it."

Adding one final piece to the "discourse of democracy" puzzle, nineteenth-century German philosopher Friedrich Hegel suggested a description of how ideas evolve through conflict resolution. First, one puts forth a proposition, a "thesis." Due to contradictions inherent in all propositions, this generates its opposite, an "antithesis," typically provided by another. Sort of a Garden of Eve–like, "This apple is bad," "No, Eve, the apple'sssss not bad, it'ssss good even." This process results in a richer idea, a "synthesis" or a justification of sorts, which both preserves and transcends the previous opposites: "The apple may be a little bad, but a bit of knowledge would be nice too." The process continues as the new and "improved" synthesis becomes the new thesis, thus evoking an antithesis of its own, and an even more shiny synthesis results. And thus the infamous Hegelian Dialectic marches on.

Accepting this as the mode of communication and evolution of ideas, it has been argued that it may be used for intellectual manipulation to coerce people to justify what may not be best for one or society (see the apple-eating heroine/villain above). Some suggest that this interplay covertly underlies a foundation for socialism: one proposes his or her own position, and then another (i.e., the government) counters it, and then—setting all differences aside—

everyone arrives at an agreement, the two views synthesized, just as "they" planned. At least you've been warned.

So go wave a flag and get your dissent on—just don't shout so loud that it hurts our ears.

MARRIAGE = 1 WOMAN + 1 MAN

Just wait until we get to the hard stuff like calculus and integration. Though in the United States, a man plus a woman also equals about a 45 percent chance of the man and woman ditching their shared plus sign and getting divorced. And with most of the concern over gay marriage coming from the religious right, it should be somewhat of a surprise that their divorce rate is *higher* than that of the non-religious atheists and agnostics. You can do the math on that one.

But this is just mathematics. Let's get caught up in semantics, shall we? Marriage, by definition, *is* (currently) between a man and a woman.

In like manner, marriage by definition in 1966 could have been accurately summarized by a bumper sticker that read, "Marriage = 2 People of the Same Race." In a court case upholding this, the trial judge proclaimed, "Almighty God created the races . . . [and] placed them on separate continents . . . [which] shows that he did not intend for the races to mix." Interracial marriage remained illegal until a 1967 Supreme Court decision ruled otherwise. Even today, Muslim women are victims of so-called honor killings in which family members or others in the community kill them for such "crimes" as interracial dating, though also for infidelity, flirting, and in some extreme cases, such as the husband having a dream that the woman betrayed him. These are often carried out publicly and even celebrated, and the United Nations estimates that approximately 5,000 occur annually.

"Semantics, shemantics," a definition-based conversation

often goes. And for good reason. It's been said (or at least repeatedly heard) that to call the tail a leg doesn't give a dog five legs. In this same vein, regardless of what we call it, it seems we should all have the same basic rights, as marriage does confer numerous advantages that unmarried couples do not have. A 2009 *New York Times* article investigated the difference in costs between two hypothetical, equally matched couples: The gay unmarried couple incurs between $41,000 and $467,000 more costs over a lifetime than the married couple, not to mention forfeiting other rights and privileges as well.

So if "a man lying with another man" truly sends the two "lie-ers" into eternal hellfire, then shouldn't we allow them to make that choice freely? After all, all of those Catholics consciously choosing divorce also commit the same level of sin—aptly termed a *mortal* sin—and no one is lobbying to make divorce illegal.

Though how soon we forget about the story of creation—as told by no one who was there—summed up in this bumper-sticker anti-wisdom:

IT WAS ADAM AND EVE NOT ADAM AND STEVE

True—*so the biblical story goes*—it was. But before we go basing public policy on such stories, we should address just a few concerns about it first to see if it's something we want to use to determine who gets to enjoy rights in our society.

If the apple really contained the "Knowledge of Good and Evil," then Adam and Eve did not know good and evil before sampling it. So it doesn't seem very fair to punish a woman for something she didn't know was not good, such as disobeying God telling her to not eat a piece of fruit. We don't morally judge infants for taking things from a friend's purse, but we do condemn older children, or praise them for not doing so. Plus, once Eve learned that her actions were not good, she immediately felt ashamed, which actually seems quite commendable. It's not like she ran around the garden afterward bragging, "How about dem apples."

And after all of that, it seems unfair and excessively harsh for everyone else—especially people not even alive at the time—to be punished for what this dynamic duo did without their even knowing they did wrong in the first place. Imagine a principal punishing the entire school as well as all *future* enrollees for two people caught doing something they didn't even know—couldn't know—was wrong. None of this seems anywhere close to what we currently value in an ethical system.

If God is all-knowing, why couldn't He find Adam after he ate the apple? And why didn't He also call out "Eve, where are you?" especially since she ate the apple to begin with?

In 2007, Nebraska state senator Ernie Chambers sued God for terrorizing humanity with widespread death. (The case was dismissed on grounds that God couldn't be properly notified, despite the senator's plea that God's omniscience should require that He knew of the lawsuit.) So couldn't God be put on trial for entrapment as well, by knowingly placing two people with no knowledge in a garden with a talking snake and a magic apple He knew they'd eat? As other bumper-sticker wisdom suggests,

EVE WAS FRAMED

After eating the apple, they both became ashamed of their bodies and invented the first fashion item, the Fig Leaf Collection. But, aside from those not ashamed of their bodies, why should we be ashamed of our bodies once we "know" about them? What do we make of God's question to Adam, "Who told you that you were naked?" It doesn't seem like that's something he needs to be told.

Now, with a clear understanding of this particular story of creation, we can move on to applying the fruits of this discussion to distributing rights in the United States. Aside from the above biblical "proof," it's been suggested that same-sex marriage will tear down the fabric of the family, devaluing marriage. James Dobson of the Christian-based *Focus on the Family* radio broadcasts clearly states, "When you confuse what marriage is, young people just don't get married." First of all, this is coming from a country in which a pop star can get married in Vegas to a man who has a child out of wedlock and another by a different woman on the way, only to have the marriage annulled two days later. In contrast, Denmark, Norway, and Sweden have all allowed gay civil unions for at least ten years, and in each of these countries not only did the heterosexual marriage rate *increase* (by upward of 25 percent in Sweden), but the divorce rate dropped. This all might be part of the motivation for the strangely harsh bumper-sticker wisdom response to Dobson from others, "Focus on Your Own Damn Family."

So yes, focus on your own family, and eat apples, and talk to snakes if you choose, that doesn't harm anybody. Though beware: They might bite you instead.

> # CAPITALISM IS THE EXTRAORDINARY BELIEF THAT THE NASTIEST OF MEN, FOR THE NASTIEST OF REASONS, WILL SOMEHOW WORK FOR THE BENEFIT OF US ALL

Nothing like a little biting rhetoric to drive home a point. And, if you're like most readers, you not only have a cursory knowledge of capitalism, but live it daily. Ironically, it looks as though some money-savvy capitalist produced a big batch of these glossy stickers and sold them at a high profit margin. Good economics.

This bumper-sticker wisdom is actually a non-attributed quote from early-twentieth-century economist John Maynard Keynes. Keynes refers to capitalists as "nasty men" simply because they act in line with their so-called nasty—i.e., selfish—reasons. Yet these very reasons drive what is often referred to as the guiding force of capitalism: "the invisible hand."

Enter Adam Smith, considered by many the Father of Economics and the thinker who provided an intellectual basis for capitalism. Smith, though, considered himself much more of a moral philosopher, studying and then teaching morality for a majority of his academic career and publishing his first book on the topic. It was in this book, *The Theory of Moral Sentiment,* where he established much of the foundational ideas for his more popularized ideas on economics. With a moral framework based on the power and influence of sympathy, he then observed the self-interested nature of humans in pursuit of money and goods—i.e., *capital.* As he later explained in his opus *An Inquiry into the Nature and Causes of the Wealth of Nations,* in our individually pursuing our respective self-interests, the ideal amount of goods—"widgets," as economists like to say of the general class of products—and economic stability will result. For example, Sally will create more valuable widgets for Emma because Sally wants to acquire as much money as she can. Likewise, Emma will do the same with regard to, say, her bread-baking skills. And the result: Capitalism's infamous "invisible hand" helps everyone acquire considerably greater goods than we otherwise would if Emma were simply baking bread as her responsibility to the state, or for Sally's sake alone. As Smith wrote, "It is not from the benevolence of the butcher, the brewer, or the baker that we expect our dinner, but from their regard to their own interest." All of this results not from "their humanity but [from] their self-love."

In short, "You be selfish. It's better for me anyway." And the response, "Yeah, well, same to you." Though some 200 years later one might wonder as to the whereabouts of this ghostlike appendage while the executives of Enron and the directors of the big banks such as Citibank leading up to America's financial crisis all pursued their self-interest. Giving a fair nod to this bumper-sticker wisdom, it's hard to see the greater goods their "hands" provided. As Nobel Prize economist Joseph Stiglitz remarks of such companies, "Adam Smith said that maximizing self-interest and social interest were coincident, and I think that sort of dramatic illustration shows that they are not." Invisible hand? There it isn't.

Keynes saw things differently. Instead of having the kids running around doing what they want, the parents should be more involved; this translates to having the government stimulating economic welfare for its citizens. This requires actions like reducing interest rates, cutting taxes, or investing in the private sector—in simple terms, the government "earns less" and spends more. While this causes the government to run at a deficit, it is the only way, he argued, to allow growth while the economy slows. This investment would prevent such long-term problems as unemployment and social duress, while avoiding economic slumps that would otherwise take years to overcome. Then, ideally (optimistically) the government can run at a surplus and repay debt in boom times. One could imagine Adam Smith's own bumper-sticker wisdom in response: **KEYNESIANISM IS THE STRANGE IDEA THAT THE KINDEST OF PEOPLE, FOR THE GREATEST OF REASONS, WILL DRIVE OUR COUNTRY INTO MASSIVE DEBT AND CALL IT GOOD.**

Lastly, in true "marketplace of ideas" fashion, we critique capitalism from the socialist camp, through the lens of its most influential advocate, Karl Marx. Marx predicted that the minority with all the money (bourgeoisie) would continue acquiring exponentially more than the majority working class (proletariat), eventually causing the proletariat to become so downtrodden and alienated that they revolt. As an alternative, Marx argued that the people should collectively own the "means of production" (i.e., all the stuff) and that everyone earn basically the same. This was fleshed out by poet Percy Bysshe Shelley, writing half a century before Marx: "The rich have become richer and the poor have become poorer," which the data confirms as well. Though still no revolt. And Smith's bumper sticker on his "other car": **SOCIALISM IS THE AS-**

TOUNDING IDEA THAT WITH EVERYONE WORKING THE SAME AND EARNING THE SAME WITH NO INCENTIVE, OUR LIVES WILL SOMEHOW BE BETTER.

That one, and MY OTHER CAR IS . . . BUILT BY INVISIBLE HANDS.

I'M ALREADY AGAINST THE NEXT WAR

It's been said "Minds are like parachutes—they only function when open." This has hardly been taken into account by this bumper-sticker wisdom. To give this bumper sticker its fair due, maybe the sticker owner has just jumped from the proverbial plane, with chute and mind still closed. He's currently thinking, "Not only am I against *this* war, I am against all war because *no conceivable state of affairs* or evil warlords committing genocide could justify it." And maybe this will change as he sees the ground quickly approaching. Or maybe, as the Chinese proverb suggests, "A closed mind is like a closed book: just a block of wood," and what makes you think a block of wood could open a parachute to begin with?

We can imagine this very sticker on Mahatma Gandhi's backpack—an "arm-sling sticker" for all those practicing the ascetic, non-materialistic lifestyle void of vehicles with bumpers. In lieu of war, Gandhi adhered to the Hindu ethic of *ahimsa,* or nonviolence. He famously amended the Bible's Old Testament philosophy of "an eye for an eye," adding the caveat "will make the whole world blind." In leading the independence movement against the warring British, he instead employed non-violent tactics such as boycotting British products, peaceful protest, and fasting.

While the Bible somewhat overturned its eye-gouging ways in Matthew's turning-the-other-cheek approach, it was St. Thomas Aquinas who made prominent a list of criteria to actually justify waging war. Still popular today, "Just War Theory" determines when one party may justifiably declare war on another; stronger yet, when this declaration is morally required. The next time two siblings go to battle, see if they pass the criteria for a just war, in which war must:

1. Occur for a just cause—"He stole my video game/toothbrush/girlfriend."
2. Be declared by proper authority—"Me." "No, *me.*"
3. Be carried out for the right intentions—"With the intent to further my cause (see [1])."
4. Have a reasonable chance for success—A fifty-pound little brother who can barely lift his backpack cannot take on big brother with a black belt in karate.
5. Have a goal proportional to the methods used—sort of a "Don't hammer a nail with a sledgehammer" clause: Big brother can't torch the other's room just to destroy a mean drawing he made.

When you sit the warring brother down, be prepared to argue for days about such vague terms as *just cause, proper authority, right intention, reasonable chance,* and *proportional objective.* By the time an intended war is finally declared as *just,* the desire for battle may subside. As our bumper-sticker wisdom confirms, maybe that next war isn't needed after all. Though, remaining in the biblical vein, then President Bush relied on the Old Testament prophesies of the Apocalypse to defend going to war. As he told France's president at the time, Jacques Chirac, "This confrontation is willed by God, who wants to use this conflict to erase His people's enemies before a New Age begins." Bush's quest to go on "a mission from God," as he also explained to the Palestinian foreign minister, may cause one to question whether we can consider him a "proper authority" for declaring war in the first place.

To give Just War Theory its fair due, and in simple terms, we can provide a justification for war on utilitarian grounds—do whatever results in the greater good. The potential positive results of war—freedom from immoral governments, for example—should outweigh the horrible evils that war elicits. The *just war* is more than simply an eye for an eye, but instead is based on the idea that by losing a few eyes future eyes won't be taken. The real question for this bumper-sticker owner: Does *any* conceivable state of affairs exist in which it would be justifiable for one country to attack another? If you side with Gandhi, then keep on sticking that sticker, but if Aquinas persuades you, there are plenty of stickers out there for you—maybe just the clichéd yet thoughtful "Practice Random Acts of Kindness."

The   GUN CONTROL   *Segment*

Along with the Christian fish symbol, the "Guns Don't Kill People" sticker is one of the most responded-to bumper stickers in existence. In 1791, the United States Constitution was amended again (hence, the Second Amendment) to allow citizens the right to keep and bear arms. At the time, "arms" included the single-shot musket that took a full minute to reload, as they didn't have handguns, automatic weapons, and rocket launchers. Then in 1927, along with Ford's Model-A car came bumpers (the earlier Model-T didn't have bumpers for stickers), thus presenting a vehicle for the ensuing conversation.

GUNS DON'T KILL PEOPLE, PEOPLE DO

GUNS DON'T KILL PEOPLE, BULLETS DO

GUNS DON'T KILL PEOPLE, DRIVERS WITH CELL PHONES DO

GUNS DON'T KILL PEOPLE, RADICALS AND PRO-LIFERS DO

GUNS DON'T KILL PEOPLE, GUNS KILL DINNER

NO . . . I'M PRETTY SURE THAT GUNS KILL PEOPLE

HEY, DUMB ASS, IT'S LACK OF PARENTING, NOT GUNS!

BLAMING GUNS FOR VIOLENCE IS LIKE BLAMING PENCILS FOR SPELLING MISTAKES

GUN CONTROL ISN'T ABOUT GUNS. IT'S ABOUT CONTROL.

GUN CONTROL MEANS USING BOTH HANDS.

2ND AMENDMENT: PROTECT IT. PRESERVE IT.

IT'S THE REPEATING CRIMINAL, NOT THE REPEATING FIREARM!

I'm glad we had this little chat.

. . . .

IT WILL BE A GREAT DAY WHEN OUR SCHOOLS GET ALL THE MONEY THEY NEED AND THE AIR FORCE HAS TO HOLD A BAKE SALE TO BUY A BOMBER

Seems like our "Free Tibet" marketers could have helped this cause in creating something a little more concise—something like "Schools Not Bombs." Or maybe they could have just loaned them the "Free" and gone with "Free Education"—that way it could be a double entendre, with public education being free for the students and also *freeing* Education from the shackles of politics and the more immediately lucrative defense industry.

In 2008, the Department of Education had a budget of $80 billion, while the Department of Defense had eight times that. No bake sales for the Air Force. But we're probably somewhat thankful for this, if not explicitly so. Living in a country relatively free from foreign attack is much better than the alternative, and probably worth paying for, so we can walk freely to these schools that we wish were nicer in the first place. Given the frenzy that resulted from the recent attack on the United States on 9/11, causing people to avoid flying—despite driving the same distance being considerably more dangerous—and embracing the "culture of fear," we probably don't want to rely on door-to-door cookie sales to fund paper tiger bombers.

Fortunately, the two aren't mutually exclusive. We can simultaneously educate and protect; we just might need to be shaken a bit to realize it. Author-turned-educator Dave Eggers is attempting to do just this. In his recent book (entitled with a bit of irony) *Teachers Have It Easy* and documentary film, he and co-authors hope to change the zeitgeist in much the same way *An Inconvenient Truth* did for the Green Movement. The authors compare the workday of a teacher to that of an actual pharmaceutical sales rep, side by side, to highlight the stark differences: By the time the sales rep has sipped his latte and met with his first doctor to convince him to use their drugs, the teacher has already met with three students separately, organized attendance rosters and lesson plans, written a quiz, met with substitute teachers, filed a textbook order, gone to a teacher meeting . . . oh, and spent an hour in the classroom with twenty-three students, motivating them and directing various projects. All for considerably less pay.

One clear solution, as this bumper-sticker wisdom suggests, is more money for salaries to hire excellent teachers. With an educated president in office following Bush, the tides have changed, with the education stimulus plan coming to fruition. Money isn't the only solution, but greater pay results in more competition. Given that nearly half of teachers quit by their fifth year due to job stress and low salary, this is a good place to start. Money may be the root of all evil, but it's also a pretty great motivator for good.

For a cool $640 billion we get safety, so what do we really *get* for all of our tax dollars in education? In any discussion of education, its value, and methodologies, one must include philosopher John Dewey, considered by many the Father of Modern Education. As a starting point in his aptly titled *Democracy and Education,* he highlights an important difference between living and non-living things in that the former "maintain themselves by renewal." Stones, when acted upon, either maintain status quo (i.e., they just "sit there") or crumble into bits. Humans, on the other hand, absorb incoming energies and can use them to their benefit, much as martial artists use the power of an assailant's jab to their own advantage. A cute metaphor, no doubt, but what now? We educate these young humans—and not in the memorize-and-regurgitate method, but in the more active manner in which we allow good critical and creative thinking to flourish—so that citizens not only come to know basic scientific and mathematical principles, but can also "share in a common life," passing judgments and discovering unique insights into human living. It is from this standpoint that a truly informed democracy can be re-born, and can flourish.

That's quite a task: not only teaching children how the world works, but inspiring them to think for themselves and become positive contributors to a democratic society. It seems that this requires more than a bake sale, though the double-fudge brownies are always a welcomed treat. We can justifiably be even more selfish, as a country of educated voters makes for a better, more fair society for everyone. It's not a surprise that Hitler once denounced universal education as "the most corroding and disintegrating poison that liberalism has ever invented for its own destruction." But fortunately for most of us, in a democratic society we can instead embrace the responsibility as stated by the more eloquent philosopher Diogenes: "The foundation of every state is the education of its youth." Safe, educated, and still time to bake and sell cookies.

It's all just fine and dandy until someone with this bumper sticker cuts you off. Literally translated "to live together," *coexist*

could also mean, more loosely, "Just get along," or even, "Collectively don't die." In light of Aristotle's insight, "Spoken words are the symbols of mental experience, and written words are the symbols of spoken words," a closer look at the symbols that take the place of the letters may prove to offer insight.

The original sticker utilizes the following symbols:

☪   Islam;

☮   Peace (somewhat redundantly, given the sticker's message);

☿   Male/female sign, thus including all known sexes of the human race and more recently used to reference transgendered individuals;

✡   Star of David for Judaism;

i   The *i* is dotted with the pentagram representing the folk-religious Paganism; it also represents Wicca, giving a nod to witches and the occult;

☯   Yin and Yang symbol for Taoism;

✝   The cross for Christianity.

Other versions of the sticker include:

The *e* (with *mc²* under it) of the relativity formula, for those viewing the world scientifically;

An *i* dotted by the Karma Wheel of Buddhism: ☸.

The intent of this sticker should be the driving force, as contradictions among these and other ideologies abound. A parody of the sticker substitutes the Communist Hammer and Sickle for the *E*, and a Nazi swastika for the *X*, highlighting the notion that one should not blindly accept all ideologies and, certainly, that not all can be completely true.

But our other options in light of this sticker are rather bleak. In lieu of "Co-*exist*," we're left with something like,

©O_®∑$† hn° ¶€Ⓐ☪e

or

©O_¶∑®*i*$h.

And while we may hope to eventually—in the distant future—"Rest in peace," and we realize that everyone will individually "Perish," the bumper-sticker wisdom here seems like the most sensible instruction—maintain your own private beliefs but just don't enforce them on everyone else. And in the meantime, we can relax in peace, ignore all of the contradictions, and enjoy the message.

THE BIG QUESTIONS

Is That Your Final Answer?

DON'T WORRY, BE HAPPY

The number of books published on happiness has increased exponentially over the past ten years, including everything from how our dogs can teach us, to what makes women happy, interviews with happy people, the science of happiness, and even how unhappiness makes us happy (stay tuned). Jeremy Bentham based his entire ethical formulation of utilitarianism on the Greatest Happiness Principle—that we ought to do that which creates the greatest happiness for the greatest number. Aristotle even centered his entire moral framework around the concept of happiness. *Eudaimonia,* he called it, in reference to a deeper sense of happiness closer to *human flourishing.* Since humans are the only species to have a "rational soul," he argued that using this reason and reasoning *well* would allow the greatest flourishing and thus achieve the happiness that we universally desire. As Thomas Jefferson purportedly asked in other bumper-sticker-style wisdom, "If ignorance is bliss why aren't people more happy?" "*Because* they're ignorant, Thomas," responds the ghost of Aristotle.

What is this stuff we're seeking to begin with? Are you happy? What about now? Now? A neuroscientist might define happiness as when serotonin pulses through one's brain. Hence, Prozac. Though this doesn't satisfy many, and forces the deeper question, Then how do I keep that stuff pulsing through my brain? Are you happy now? Psychologist Abraham Maslow developed a ranking of five classes of needs in which, as each is met, we become more and more satisfied. At the lowest rank are our biological needs such as food and water, and at the top is the need for self-actualization—doing what we were "born to do." So you just need to climb the ladder en route to that discovery. Are you happy now? Likely not, as the influential Taoist Chuang Tzu warned: "Perfect happiness is the absence of striving for happiness." For the Taoist, things come in pairs, so with happiness comes sorrow, and important here, with sorrow comes happiness. Once you realize the harmony of the two, you can embrace sorrow, likely alleviating a lot of stress and, ironically almost, becoming even happier. Worry a little, it's okay, necessary even. Happy now?

Internal pain and sadness are like the psychological version of a painful abrasion to the physical body. When cut, you focus awareness and attention to the wound. Likewise, sadness can increase one's awareness of the inner self, causing one to focus attention inward and delve deeper. These messages force us to reexamine who we are. We do this at the cost of having to sometimes lie during the umpty-ump daily encounters when we're asked by passersby to check in: "I'm doing well, you?" "I'm good, thanks." "Fine. Fine. Fine. Everything's fine." How you doing?

Shifting hemispheres to the story of Adam and Eve, author Eric Wilson explains in his counterculture book *Against Happiness* that after "falling" and eating the pernicious Apple, they had their first encounter with true goodness. They recognized this only in the face of evil: "Only after the fall could they know, deep down, what joy was." Talk about seeing the silver lining. He continues, concerned about those who "desire only happiness in a world undoubtedly tragic," that this shallow happiness causes one to become inauthentic. Especially today, with positive psychologists preaching the rat race of happiness 24/7, people develop the survival skill of hiding behind a painted smile, ignoring the real complexities of the world and the insecurities of the inner self. They "don inauthenticity as a mask, a disguise protecting them from the abyss." Oh, great, so not only are we not happy, but now we're inauthentic too. His bumper sticker would read something more along the lines of "Don't Worry—Or Worry If You're Worried. Be Happy. Or Not." So how's it going now?

The good news: We have an inalienable right, provided by the Declaration of Independence, to the pursuit of happiness. Unfortunately they didn't go one step further and provide a right to actually *acquiring* happiness—though that would require a tax hike that not even the most impassioned liberal would support. But after deeper reflection it looks like we can take the pressure off a little.

You happy now? If not, don't worry.

NOTHING MATTERS WHEN . . .

. . . you're dancing, you're fishing, you're in love with a Jersey Girl. The list goes on and on. Clearly things do matter, regardless of the driver looking for fish or going on dates with girls from Jersey. Why else would he do such things in the first place? Which should cause one to wonder if maybe nothing matters regardless of what one does. As it turns out, *nothing*—the actual *lack of something*—truly does matter in a very real way. We really should make much ado about it.

To begin with, since the moment you were born, you have benefited from one of the most important institutions we have, based completely on nothing—your right to life. In doing so, you have consistently done your corresponding duty, known as a "negative" duty in that it requires one to do nothing, thus providing your friends and fellow citizens with that same right. Well done. Nothing matters.

One of the most popular sitcoms in history, *Seinfeld,* boasted of its being about nothing, with entire episodes devoted to such nothingness as waiting to be seated at a restaurant or searching for a car in a parking garage. The show's DVD collection includes notes entitled "Notes About Nothing," and the characters in the show even propose a show about "nothing" exactly like the one viewers are already watching. The character Jerry imagines how the pitch to NBC would transpire: "They say, 'What's your show about?' I say 'Nothing,' " and after George confirms this, Jerry responds, "I think you may have something here." But in the final episode, the four main characters all view a man being robbed and they do nothing about it (aside from telling a few jokes). They are sentenced to jail for breaking the Good Samaritan law in Massachusetts, as their immoral nothingness morphed them into Bad Samaritans. Unfortunately, this situation has earned the proper name of the "Genovese Syndrome" in reference to a woman in New York who was brutally murdered and none of the *thirty-eight* viewers from adjacent apartments did anything—more aptly, they did nothing. Nothing matters.

Nothing matters more than "nothing" to religions in the Far East and India, such as Taoism, Hinduism, and Buddhism. The Buddhist's ultimate goal of Nirvana is best summarized by *nothing*. Literally translated as "snuffed out," the aim is to extinguish one's ego and worldly desires to achieve a deep peace of mind and thus a connection with the Oneness of the universe. Kind of like being in a deep sleep while you're awake. Nothing matters.

The Taoist also celebrates nothing as much as they do *something*, for in this tradition, opposites are necessary: their response to the Western "No Pain, No Gain" is more along the lines of "No Pain, No Pleasure." Lao Tzu explains, "Clay is molded to form a utensil / But it is on its non-being that the utility of the utensil depends." The spoon acquires its utility due to the *nothing* with which we scoop our soup. When Gandhi and his followers adhered to the principle of non-violence (*ahimsa*) through peaceful protest and boycott, this not only prevented the whole world from going blind, but eventually freed India from British oppression. Nothing mattered.

Back in the Western world, we have a real bias against nothing, despite the fact that doing nothing is important in many areas of life. Data shows that professional soccer goalies in penalty-kick situations consistently guess and jump to one side even though staying in the center of the goal provides considerably better odds at stopping the shot. It turns out they would rather look like they did something and fail, than do nothing and fail less. Because nothing matters.

It looks like one *can* get something from nothing, despite what physicists say. Socrates was really on to something in his infamous "The wise man is he who knows that he knows nothing." While speaking ironically, his knowledge of his own ignorance—his knowing nothing—fulfilled the Oracle's prophecy that he was wisest of them all. Then again, if Socrates enjoyed fishing or dated a Jersey girl, maybe nothing wouldn't have mattered so much to him.

LIFE IS JUST LIKE A STRAW—IT SUCKS

This witty pessimist provides a good instance of a *dis*-analogy. A straw doesn't *do* anything. To be more apt, this bumper sticker would have to say "Life GETS SUCKED." Though someone experiencing the existential angst that life sucks probably isn't thinking as clearly, and certainly not as rigidly logically, as they could.

We can examine their most likely intended point: Life in general is just plain bad. Yet, here we encounter the unavoidable issue in any investigation involving a value-claim: relativity. "Compared to what?" we ask. For example, when our same disparaging bumper-sticker owner announces, "This pizza sucks," it is in comparison to other pizza (or, at least, other food). It is similar to our assigning "strangeness" to the universe—strange compared to what? It's the only universe we know.

Maybe, then, at the least he means "*My* life sucks," as he has been wrapped up in that famous pastime of ours in which we compare our lives with our neighbors, constantly keeping up with those infamous Joneses and all of their Pollyannaish bumper stickers. Though in that case, the bumper-sticker wisdom wouldn't be quite so universal, much in the same way we're uninterested in the answer to the not-so-pressing question "What is the meaning of Joe's life?"

Our remaining option is that life—that is, being alive—sucks in comparison to the "no life" option. If our aforementioned Joe answers the "meaning of Joe's life" question along the lines of "There is none, my life does suck," he's now welcome to file a "Wrongful Birth" lawsuit. In this amazing legal maneuver, he can sue his parents and their doctors for allowing him to even be born to experience the suckiness in the first place.

But to address the overarching question, the angst referenced earlier is a prime subject of existentialism, which deals directly with the "meaning of life" question. A core tenet of existentialism is the notion that we are truly, deeply free; as existentialist Jean-Paul Sartre wrote, "Existence precedes essence"—we are born and *then* choose to become who we are. Thus, we cannot rightly blame (or praise) our DNA, our upbringing, some predetermined fate, a "dark past," nor any cosmic forces for our lot in life. This puts the responsibility for our lives directly in our own hands. It causes feelings of dissonance (i.e., angst) as we realize that we both author our lives through our choices deeply our own, and yet, in the grand scheme of the cosmos, these choices don't matter. So with no predetermined meaning and this "angst" we experience by just being alive, the deeper meaning of life arises from what it is that we alone discover. We choose our own meaning, and there *is* meaning to be had after all.

Unfortunately for this un-grammatical, milkshake-drinking savant, he's sucked one too many straws to notice the deliciousness on just the other side.

EVEN PEOPLE WHO BELIEVE EVERYTHING IS PREDESTINED LOOK BEFORE THEY CROSS THE STREET

Of course. But they have no choice, right? It was written in the stars, "in the cards," as it were. Destined for greatness, or at least for crossing streets safely.

The really fun thing about discussing predestination is that it appears to the uninitiated as though it's completely impossible to disprove. Let's see . . . *Aspofijas;dfla k;sdfpaoyh mbmqerpot asdg opofmwa f'oa;ih ga.goeg, sdl;f a rpoanga ag;oiaj sdg os.* No mystical force or supernatural being would ever predetermine an author to write such nonsense, especially if the writer planned to have it published with a reputable publisher in the hope of acquiring thousands and thousands of readers. This is true martyrdom on behalf of free will. And how creative, writing something never before created. That must be the doing of "free will."

But the predeterminist quickly responds that some force, likely unknown, caused or at least compelled the author to do such a radical act. The author was destined to do it even before he was born. So obviously, then, "looking before they cross the street" doesn't disprove predestination. Not by these standards at least.

There's an important distinction to be made between predestination and determinism. A trip to the ice cream store should help illustrate this:

> *Predestined:* From the moment you were born—even before that—you would end up in *this* ice cream store on *this* day and "choose" bubblegum flavor.
> *Free will:* You chose bubblegum ice cream just because you wanted to.
> *Determined:* Your genetics and environment control your choice of ice cream flavors. Since these are both out of

your control and are the only factors guiding your action, then choosing bubblegum ice cream was not truly free.

While the doctrine of predestination is not necessarily a religious doctrine, Christian Calvinism is most responsible for its popularity. As God is all-knowing, he knows for a fact that you will order bubblegum ice cream and thus, you can't *not*. And since God is Creator and Author, He literally built all actions into his plan, much like the director of a movie does for his actors: "And then he asserts, 'I'll have bubblegum ice cream, please.' Cut, that's a wrap!"

This worldview can be seductively alluring. If it is all in God's hands, then one is truly along for the ride. No need to sweat the small stuff. And when something goes wrong, one's provided with an opportunity to play the "Why would God do that?" game.

But some interesting complexities arise. How could we assign moral blame (or praise) if none of the blameworthy actions were our choosing? As the first known "determinist lawyer," Clarence Darrow argued that criminals do not truly deserve their incarceration and are only in jail "on account of circumstances which are entirely beyond their control and for which they are in no way responsible." Without free will we could not punish people because they "deserved" it. Instead it would be more like the way the futuristic police in the movie *Minority Report* do, where they arrest people for crimes they are *about* to commit. And what then motivates us for pursuit of the afterlife if these slots were determined before we were even born, as God says in John 15:15: "You did not choose Me but I chose you"? So one is faced with either the psychological angst of failing to earn the privilege of being one of God's "chosen ones," or the rationalization of spending one's entire life as a mere puppet of some Grand Puppeteer.

Advocates of free will often rely on the fact that, for any freely chosen action, they *could have done otherwise*. In choosing bubblegum ice cream, they could have chosen another flavor, or none at all. In response, the determinist often agrees, but adds one nagging yet undeniable fact: You *didn't* do otherwise—*you did what you did*. So the determinist's argument goes, had the situation been different—had you a different brain composition or were you in a different environment—then you would have chosen differently, but your decision and action resulted from (i.e., was determined by) these factors and forces out of your immediate control. Not much room for free will there.

Recent brain scans reveal that, with regard to seemingly freely chosen actions, the brain actually starts the cascade of movement *before* the conscious will kicks in. Our brain makes the decision and milliseconds later we engage our feeling of free will. This is great news for baseball batters and other sportspersons, because were the batter to take time to decide to swing at the ball, it would be too late. It is that pesky *feeling* of free will that provides so much distress for the budding philosopher. As the English author Samuel Johnson wrote, "All theory is against the freedom of the will; all experience is for it." Seventeenth-century philosopher Baruch Spinoza once suggested that if a stone could think, it would fancy itself freely acting in the same way that an infant believes that it freely desires milk. He reminds us of our ignorance as to the actual causes of our own desires. Only recently, with the advent of neuroscience, have we begun to discover these causes.

So, feel "free" to choose which theory drives your selection of ice cream. But, for whatever reason, look both ways before crossing the street to get there.

TRY TO BE ALIVE. YOU'LL BE DEAD SOON ENOUGH.

That's the thing: Of all the things you know, you *know* you exist. This is the brilliance of René Descartes's oft-quoted "I think therefore I am." What did he prove? He proved that some thinking, doubting thing—"I," for lack of a better term—exists. Not you. Not me. Not even René Descartes, with arms and legs and published books. At that point in his illustrious *Meditations* he hadn't done anything else. But he did prove absolute knowledge, for something must be there to do the thinking and doubting. So at the least, we can *know* that "I" exists, in some form or another, TBD.

There is more to know. Obviously. Philosophers have come a long way since the time of Socrates, whose greatest contribution was "I know only one thing, that I do not know." But when we talk about Truth (capital *T* absolute Truth), that "I" exists is a starting place that we can all—Democrat, Republican, religious, atheist—agree on.

So why not "Try to be alive"? "Get busy living, or get busy dying," as the wrongly convicted hero of *The Shawshank Redemption* urges. This presents one with the opportunity to refute the overt pessimist's vision of life being all about death: As soon as we're born, we start dying. Not so, if you adhere to the bumper-sticker wisdom laid out here.

Take this simple example. When you walk into a store that has just opened for the day, you wouldn't say they were *closing*, despite the fact that, with every minute that passes, they get closer to closing. The store is simply *open*. But imagine entering the same store in the late afternoon as the owner has started sweeping up, cashing out the register, and locking the back door. "Hey, shopkeep, why are you locking the back door?" you ask. *"We're closing,"* he responds. They're not closing until they *decide* to close. "See you next time," you say to keep his spirits up.

Unfortunately, in life, we don't know if we'll *see you next time*. We don't even know when we'll be "closed," but we do get to decide when we're "closing." And you don't even have to lock up because when your shop closes, you're closed for good—as far as we know.

REMEMBER WHO YOU WANTED TO BE

Knock knock.
Who's there?
You.
You, *who*?
You, who? Exactly.

First, you need to figure out who *you* are. Your *identity*. In part this depends on who you were. Then you can determine if this bumper-sticker wisdom is really worth pursuing.

Before you embark, a quick warning. David Hume argues that any concept of self and identity that we assign to ourselves is fictitious—more of a convenient place-holder than anything else. And pretty much all Buddhists agree with him, believing there to be no permanent self. They attribute our delusion as being caused by our assigning names to things, and to ourselves. A name, as the Buddhist story goes, is just "a label, a convenient designation, or a mere name . . . In the absolute sense there is no self here to be found."

Think about Bess, the computer you've owned for ten years. Since the time you bought it, you've gradually changed every part of it: the hard drive, then the outer casing, the screen, and finally a new keyboard to replace the one you wore out writing your last novel. *Nothing* about it is the same, but you still call it ol' Bess, the computer you've owned for ten years. In some sense, you've been deceived by that name and, while convenient, you now realize that it fails to capture the deeper reality. Now go stand in front of the mirror holding your newborn baby picture—even wear your birthday suit for added effect. Who are you, anyway? (Seriously.)

Regardless of whether you're the *same* person or not, you certainly *are* someone—You read, therefore you are. How do you decipher who that is? Are you the waiter at the local restaurant? Yes, but only two days a week. Though what if you work there seven days a week? Now you are a waiter more than you are anything else in your life (just do the math). Clearly you act differently serving others at the restaurant than you do in your "real" life. You are just acting, playing a role. But when, in life, does the acting stop and the *being* begin? Jean-Paul Sartre writes, "I see myself because somebody sees me," and this causes one to act a certain way. Comedian Chris Rock takes Sartre one step further, noting, "When you go out on a date with someone, you are not meeting them, you are meeting their representative." And likewise for numerous situations such as interviews, cocktail parties, and most other times somebody sees you.

But this mental trick—trying to behave in a way that you know you are truly not, or wish you were—causes angst. It's like the college student who sits in his Psychology of Advertising class, mocking the practically nude Abercrombie clothing models, yet wearing their pants and a Ralph Lauren Polo shirt. This deeper sense of self-deception is what Sartre calls acting in "bad faith." We spend a lot of our time trying to make our actions fit with our concept of our identity, instead of just letting our actions create our identity.

Are you considerate because you hold the door for strangers? Or do you hold the door for strangers because you're considerate? Aristotle argues the former in his famous quote "You are what you repeatedly do." Sartre agrees, claiming that we shape our identity, and not the other way around—that our existence precedes our essence. So, no more pleading, "I couldn't help it. That's just who I am." You make your identity, it doesn't make you. This should be good news.

So if you do remember who you wanted to be, and you're not that today, and still wish you were, then go be that person. Or just stop trying-to-be someone and just *be*. Start holding the door for strangers, if you so choose.

I BELIEVE IN LIFE BEFORE DEATH

Life after death? Who knows—impossible to say, really. Life before death? That seems like something about which we can be absolutely certain. If not, then something seriously *Matrix*-like is going on, but even then, it's life before death. This bumper-sticker owner likely goes beyond mere "belief" in life before death and actually *knows* of it, though the play on "life after death" has not gone unnoticed.

In life we can either act on what we *know* or on what we *don't know* (*but maybe wish were so*), the latter option nicely summarized by the King James Bible: "Faith is the substance of things hoped for." When we *know* one thing and literally *guess* at others—Was I around *before* my birth? Will I be around *after* my death?—most find it prudent to embrace the knowledge-stuff and let the chips fall where they may.

In some ways, it boils down to a gamble of sorts. To set the stage, imagine playing roulette in which the wheel has thirty-six black and red slots and, on the French version, one green slot (as opposed to the American version, containing two): If gambling one dollar, with the payoff for a red slot at two dollars while the green pays back a thousand, one would be wise to bet green, even though the odds of landing on that are low.

French mathematician Blaise Pascal has us imagine a gamble in which the payoff is even better: You gamble your current life. The payoff for *not* believing in God is living that life as you choose, but the payoff *for* believing in God is infinite happiness in the afterlife. As an added incentive, if you bet against God and it turns out that He/She/It exists, then you are tortured infinitely.

And here's the kicker: You can't just walk out of Pascal's Casino as in our previous roulette case. As he reminds us, "You must wager. It is not optional. You are embarked." You either believe or you don't. "Not choosing" is not an option in the God Casino. As popular Canadian rock trio Rush sings, "If you chose not to decide you still have made a choice."

Mathematically, your finite years are nothing in the face of infinity. The case is clear even for a female in Macau, having the world's longest average life expectancy of a mere eighty-eight years. Any finite gain in life—having guilt-free sex before marriage a few times, for example, or going out for drinks with friends, working on the Sabbath, etc.—is a mathematical *zero* in light of the possibility, however small, of infinite rewards. All those math classes, finally paying off.

But we must turn a quick *what-if* eye toward Pascal and wonder, "What if I've never even heard of the *winning god* who actually exists?" As Richard Dawkins reminds us, "We are all atheists about most of the gods that societies have ever believed in." Just which of the hundreds of supernatural beings do we wager on, and what if It ends up being a jealous god who exists (i.e., "Thou shalt worship no other gods but me.") but we wagered on the wrong one? As cartoon philosopher Homer Simpson rationalizes his way out of mass, "Suppose we've chosen the wrong god. Every time we go to church we're just making him madder and madder."

And finally, you gasp, "What if I just can't do it?" Envision this simple task we'll call "Bowen's Gamble":

If you decide to believe that the earth is flat, you win one billion dollars.

Clearly the prudent option is to believe in the flat earth. "But I can't get myself to believe in, um, something I don't believe," you respond, desperately, to the tune of Freud's comment, "No one can be forced into belief." To this, Pascal frighteningly instructs us to "renounce reason," "deaden our acuteness," and realize "nothing is certain . . . for it is not certain that we may see tomorrow."

But we *do* see today.

THE ONLY THINGS CERTAIN IN LIFE ARE DEATH AND TAXES

You say it—or, should I say, *stick it*—like it's a bad thing. First of all, on the whole taxes issue, wouldn't you much rather have someone else out there building roads for you to drive on, regulating your food and drugs, and defending you against attack on a daily basis while you go for a walk and have tea with friends after work? This likely explains why most Americans went to work on Tax Day 2009, willingly allotting some percentage of that day's earnings to taxes. As that other bumper sticker reads,

TAXES ARE THE PRICE OF CIVILIZATION

Interestingly, thousands of others were out protesting at one of the hundreds of the nationwide "(Neo) Boston Tea Parties," with some even sponsored by Fox "News." They waited eight years while the Bush administration nearly doubled the country's $5.7 trillion debt, and then spent one day throwing out tea bags in protest. While the original Tea Party revolted against taxation *without* representation (clearly not the case now), the current-day TEA-partiers devised a clever acronym for their party: Taxed Enough Already. Ironically, the tea-baggers bought millions of tea bags that they then disposed of in protest of *wasteful spending*—all at a time in history with a new president in office who had actually lowered taxes for a majority.

Having dissolved the concern of the latter, what's to say about the former? A lot, actually. The great Socrates was sentenced to death for "corrupting the youth"—basically for asking questions of boastful politicians highlighting their ignorance where they instead claimed knowledge. No questioning policy decisions and

TEA parties for that era. He then willingly drank of the poisonous hemlock when he could instead have fled into hiding.

Death, he reasoned, is either "A state of nothingness and utter unconsciousness"—which would not *be* anything, or if something, a great night's sleep and thus, "an unspeakable gain"—*or*, in death, as some suggest, "there is a change and migration of the soul from this world to another," in which case Socrates gets to hang out with Odysseus, Sisyphus, and others with whom to converse and where, he delights, "They do not put a man to death for asking questions," especially since, at that point, you're immortal to begin with. Not too shabby either.

In sum, Socrates claims that fearing death is silly, because you really don't know what's coming down the pike, and the options really aren't that bad. To claim to know what's next for you is "ignorance of a disgraceful sort," in which you claim to know what you can't.

Mark Twain adds a further point to this footnote of Socrates: "I do not fear death. I had been dead for billions and billions of years before I was born, and had not suffered the slightest inconvenience from it." So why all the fuss now over the next billion years, when no fuss over the previous billion? You already missed out on the dinosaurs, the first Olympic Games, and the Britney Spears of the prehistoric era. Do you really need to be around when present-day Britney Spears becomes president and we finally find a way to build apartments on Mars?

Death expert—yes, the niche has been filled—Ernst Becker explains the psychological underpinnings of your affirmative answers to these questions. Not only do humans feel special, as though the world, nay the universe, *needs* us and was meant to have us in it, but this hubris transfers to the individual: *you*. It's nicely summed up by the ancient wisdom "Luck is when the guy next to you gets hit by the arrow." Though we also see it in religious perspective, as one proclaims a heaven-sent miracle from an allegedly *all-loving* God when a child survives a tsunami that killed 200,000 others (I'll leave it to the reader to distill the irony). Interestingly, if one truly believes that their deceased loved ones are headed for eternal bliss, we should expect nothing short of rejoicing upon their passing away, though this is usually far from the case.

Becker explains that humans—little survival machines—are narcissistic by nature. So we form a hero-complex to justify our sense of "cosmic specialness, of ultimate usefulness to creation, of unshakable meaning." But heroes never die—see Superman, Batman, Wonder Woman, et al.—so this whole Dying Hero thing doesn't really jibe with us and makes us anxious. We justify it all by at least leaving our mark: writing a book or something so we can achieve worldly immortality. I'm a hero after all.

So, in the end, you can't be certain of taxes because millions don't pay them to begin with (along with those under eighteen); and you can't be certain of death because, as some say, *you* never die but just keep living in different ways. Secondly, these can't be the only claims to certainty in life, can they? As Woody Allen suggests, "What if everything is an illusion and nothing exists? In that case, I definitely overpaid for my carpet." And lastly, as we recognize upon further examination, death and taxes aren't so bad after all. So get to work, go meet your friends, and put the tea bag in your cup of water and enjoy while there's still time.

GOT PURPOSE?

Or as the French might say, "Got *raison d'être*?" It seems that when writing a book on religion or philosophy, as an unwritten rule you must ask "What is the purpose of life?" at least once. Because it simply can't be that "Life" has no purpose. Then again . . . What is the purpose of love? And of joy? Of death, even? And what of the purpose of gravity? Or of spiders having eight legs?

The "purpose question" falls into the same trap as the never-ending search for life's "meaning," in that it's really not posing a proper question in the first place. As author Thomas Pynchon noted, "If they can get you asking the wrong questions they don't have to worry about the answers." Answers to questions of the formula "What is the meaning of *x*?" seem unattainable. "What is the meaning of pencil?" elicits either confusion or, more likely, the respondent answers the *purpose* question: "It's for writing." Wittgenstein preempts Pynchon's insight in offering his own: "If a question can be framed at all, it is also *possible* to answer it." What possible answer could suffice to the question "What is the meaning of . . . " or "What is the purpose of . . . life?"

How exhausting, constantly searching for such an intellectual chimera. Imagine asking, "What's the purpose of this?" every time you did anything. "Dad, what's the purpose of watching baseball?" "Honey, what's the purpose of our kissing like this?" One clear problem lies in the fact that this question forces one to find a general purpose—in our case here, some purpose to "life" in general. It's hard to imagine what that could even be, exactly.

The Dalai Lama suggests that life's purpose is to be happy. And to do this, we must care for the happiness of others. Aristotle agrees somewhat, though suggests that we should seek that which is desirable for its own sake, as opposed to something done for the sake of another goal. This encapsulates our intuition in which we tend to value someone who does their job because they truly love it instead of the person who works only for the paycheck. Aristotle suggests that one achieves true *flourishing* once one arrives at the final "Why?" in pursuit of why he or she does something, thus achieving the highest good. Think of the inquisitive child constantly asking "Why?"—Why must I go to school? Why do I need good grades? Why do we need knowledge? At some point, he does something for its own sake—takes a philosophy course in college, maybe, just because he desires the intrinsic value of knowledge, and nothing else. Just because. Aristotle suggests that to find the path to *excellence* in life, we should rely on that which humans do uniquely well: reason. Through employing our unique capacity to reason we achieve excellence and, thus, our *raison d'être*.

Here still we examine "life" as a general concept, when what we really want is something more specific—the purpose of *my* life. If you find a trophy in your grandparents' attic, you don't ask,

"What is the purpose of a trophy?" but instead, "What is the purpose of *this* trophy?" And we likely want the same from our "purpose of life" question.

This is where purpose and meaning intersect, despite their often merging as synonyms. The *purpose* of something may have nothing to do with its meaning and vice versa. The trophy may have served the purpose of rewarding the winners, but maybe has *meaning* in that it's the only thing of your grandmother's that you possess. You could even use the trophy for a purpose other than that for which it was intended—as a tool to reach something on a shelf, maybe—and it would be wrong of someone to claim that you shouldn't use the trophy for that supposedly unintended purpose.

Despite this, some still protest "My life won't have a purpose if humans just evolved and I have no creator to tell me what to do." But you *do* have a creator, two actually: your mom and dad. So if that's truly how you determine your life's purpose, then simply ask your parents why they created you and then do what they tell you (work on the farm, share their love, etc.). Likely, you'll find that you don't really need or even want some other being telling you what your own purpose is and determining your so-called meaning.

Many others of a similar, typically religious, ilk respond that life can have purpose and meaning only if one continues living after their body dies, in some sort of afterlife. Yet this intuition exactly opposes what happens in our actual lives. After attending a funeral or watching *Dead Poets Society,* people often come away with a deeper feeling of *carpe*-ing the *diem,* having acquired a newfound quest for living a more full, enriching life. Unfortunately, this phrase is taken almost literally as it usually lasts about as long as that particular *diem* until one is thrust back into the daily grind of minutiae. And when a patient is diagnosed with a terminal illness, the now more explicitly finite days *increase* in value, if anything: He or she avoids life's menial tasks and attends to their own respective "Bucket List," visiting new places and spending time with loved ones. In the movie *The Game,* a company can be hired by friends of those who have lost the luster for life in which they experience a near-death scenario to remind them, in a sense, that only finite days remain and to make the most of them. As the law of diminishing returns reminds us, the more one has of a particular thing, the less value each individual thing comes to hold. Thus, in the *infinite* days scenario, one could surely waste a few—even a lifetime's worth—and still lose little to nothing. The fewer days, the *more* meaning.

So with "What's the meaning of life?" being a bogus question, what we really want is the answer to the purpose question. And that is up to the owner of that thing: in this case, each respective "you." One has complete authorship of his or her own life's purpose: as part of the journey of being alive. As another bumper-sticker wisdom suggests,

THE PURPOSE OF LIFE IS A LIFE OF PURPOSE

To this point, the Greek gods, in their not so infinite wisdom, attempted to mete out the harshest of punishments to a fellow named Sisyphus. They condemned him to rolling a heavy rock up a hill only to have it immediately roll back down. Repeat. Ad infinitum. All that work and struggle for no external reward. Existential philosopher Albert Camus, in his finite wisdom, believed that we should consider Sisyphus happy: "The struggle itself towards the heights is enough to fill a man's heart." Through this lens, we might imagine the harsher punishment of a life with no purpose, as opposed to the purpose afforded Sisyphus for eternity. And if you have nowhere to start, try out this bumper-sticker wisdom to see what you think:

WHAT IF THE HOKEY POKEY IS WHAT IT'S ALL ABOUT?

Unlikely, but still fun to shake it all about.

THE AFTER-STICKER: YOU CAN READ THIS

TO BE—IN A CAVE—OR NOT TO BE, THAT IS THE QUESTION

Plato invited us to imagine that we were all born into a cave, chained down, coming to know only the shadows cast on the wall by a fire as our perceived reality. He urged us to break free from the shackles binding us to our cave of false reality and to forge through the initially blinding yet ultimately illuminating light of Truth that awaits outside. Many see this as the primary job of the philosopher or, more inclusively, the self-aware citizen. As Plato also encouraged us in our exodus from the cave: "Know thyself." But with Truth's ever-so-elusive nature, might it be the case that when we leave one cave, we simply enter another, albeit one better illuminated than the last? That is, with complete knowledge of the self and of the universe being more of an ideal than a reality, the committed truth-seeker may just be opening doors to newer and brighter caves, but caves nonetheless. The tiger born and raised in the zoo doesn't know to long for the jungle of his ancestors. But unlike the tiger, humans have the blessing—or is it a curse?—of self-awareness and imagination in communion with a dissonant quest for comfort.

As infants we inhabit a very limited, constricting cave—more of a den of sorts: one that includes a smattering of round objects and a small subset of noises and other sensory information. Eventually, just as a snake sheds its withered skin for more resilient attire, we too exchange that reality for a richer yet still deficient cave. While certainly comfortable, as if living the "dog's life" for which many working adults yearn, when we leave one cave for another, we reflect and appreciate the mirage we once inhabited, stage by stage, cave by cave. This continues for most until, at some point, we cease and settle.

Likewise on a larger, societal scale. Throughout history, humans have collectively shared various caves. Aptly named cavemen not only literally lived in caves, but through the lens of our metaphor were shackled much more tightly than we, lacking knowledge of the mechanics of the universe, of the human mind, and of countless other phenomena. How could they possibly explain rainbows, a starlit night, or the death of a compatriot? Through various "Ages"—Dark, Middle, Discovery, Enlightenment, Information—we too shed one den for other larger, more well lit caverns, and on and on. The advent of newly acquired knowledge gave us the courage to leave the comfort of our respective caves. We occupied the center of the universe for quite a while, providing great consolation for ourselves, until we became startled by the light of the fact that we live on just another planet, one of many—thousands even—and were knocked off our pedestal.

Clearly, then, we should avoid any hubris that suggests we have finally arrived outside of The Cave, with no further exploring required. We should not bemoan this admission but instead celebrate it. In a sense, these caves are all we have. And they do provide comfort. The real challenge lies in how to balance this contentment with the quest for getting to the mouth of the cave: for an exit, or more psychologically compelling, an entrance. Just as the fish cannot cognize being in the water, we too cannot fully fathom all and everything. Not yet, anyway. So we value open-mindedness, travel, education, authentic discourse, and novel experiences because, in a sense, they provide prime opportunities to explore parts of our inner and outer caves still unseen by our inquisitive eye.

These activities jolt us from our comfort—our cave-fort—zone. And when we do arrive home, in our dwelling, we will know that we have shed as much light as one can shed. This, it seems, should be comfort enough.

The twenty-first-century caveman—and with the recent light of gender equity, cave*person*—has no choice but to dwell in a cave of his or her own. Look around a bit. You may discover things in your cave you didn't know were there or you may just see a bit of light peeking through up ahead. We are standing on the shoulders of previous self-reflecting cave dwellers who have not had as great an opportunity as we do to embrace the privilege:

IF YOU CAN READ THIS . . . KNOW THY CAVE